Contents

WITHDRAWN FROM
THE LIBRARY

UNIVERSITY OF
WINCHESTER

£6.95

Literary Criticism

A Glossary of Major Terms

Patrick Murray

LONGMAN

KA 0053235 5

First published 1978 by
Smurfit Books Limited
P.O. Box 43A
Ballymount Road
Walkinstown
Dublin 12

and

Longman Group Limited
Longman House
Burnt Mill
Harlow Essex U.K.

Published in the United States of
America by Longman Inc. New York

© Smurfit Books Limited 1978
All rights reserved. No part of this
publication may be reproduced, stored
in a retrieval system, or transmitted in
any form or by any means, electronic,
mechanical, photo-copying, recording, or
otherwise, without the prior permission
of the copyright owner.

First published 1978
by Longman Group Limited
Fourth impression 1982

ISBN 0 582 35247 9

British Library Cataloguing in Publication Data

Murray, Patrick, b. 1935
    Literary criticism.
    1. Literature — Terminology
    I. Title
    803   PN44.5   78-40540

    ISBN 0-582-35247-9

KING ALFRED'S COLLEGE
WINCHESTER

801.95
MUR
54538

Printed in Singapore by
The Print House Pte Ltd.

Preface

There are many handbooks offering definitions of literary terms. Most of these are comprehensive in that they range from major general topics such as tragedy, comedy, irony and satire to the numerous minor terms traditionally used to describe matters of local detail (alliteration, assonance, zeugma, and so forth).

The present book does not attempt to compete with or supplement such works. It has been written in the belief that an extended treatment of the comparatively small number of major terms is likely to be more useful to potential users of books of this kind than a sketchy account of a much greater number, minor as well as major. Minor terms are discussed here only where they are related to the major generic ones – synedoche and metonymy appear in the article on metaphor, hyperbole and litotes in the one on irony.

The aim throughout has been to provide more than an accurate definition of each term. I have tried to show how the terms I have chosen to discuss actually work, and, where necessary, to distinguish between the modern and traditional understanding of certain terms.

The scope of the book is virtually limited to the treatment of terms relating to poetry and drama. Even in the case of terms with a wider application (the greater number of those discussed, in fact), almost all the illustrations have been drawn from poems and plays. Only in the case of allegory has extensive reference been made to works of prose fiction. The decision to limit the range of reference in this way was a conscious one. A much larger book than this would be needed if the major terms commonly used in critical discussion of prose fiction were to receive adequate treatment.

Everybody who embarks upon a work of this kind must inevitably lean on his predecessors in the field. I have found M. H. Abrams' *Glossary of Literary Terms: The Methuen Critical Idiom* series, and the Routledge *Dictionary of Modern Critical Terms* (ed. Roger Fowler) particularly useful.

This book is an introduction. Those who wish to embark on

a more extensive study of the terms will find suitable material in the bibliographies. With very few exceptions, the works cited in these bibliographies are available in modern paperback editions.

Patrick Murray

Allegory

We resort to allegory when we describe a subject under the guise of some other subject which has apt and suggestive resemblances to the first one. Allegory is often described as extended metaphor or extended simile, since it is a representation conveying a meaning other than, and in addition to, the literal meaning. Most people, when they think of allegory, think of a literary work. Confining our attention for the moment to literary allegory, we might say that if we read a story and conclude that under its surface meaning another meaning may be discovered, and that this other meaning is the *raison d'être* of the story, then we may safely decide that we have been reading an allegorical work. The allegorical author's formula runs something like, 'By this, I also mean that'. The Renaissance critic Puttenham gives a simple example, declaring that allegory is present 'if we call the Commonwealth a ship, the Prince a Pilot, the Counsellors mariners, the Storms wars'.

An allegory need not be a literary work. It may, for example, be addressed to the eye, and may be embodied in painting or sculpture. Boitcelli's *Primavera* is a famous allegorical painting. The female figure of Justice, blindfolded and carrying a scales, is allegorical. There is a kind of allegory called the Emblem. This enjoyed a considerable vogue in the sixteenth and seventeenth centuries, and featured a drawing conveying a moral lesson, accompanied by a verse which commented on its significance. Allegory can take the form of a pageant. A distinguished foreign guest may be entertained by a procession of figures representing abstractions: Peace, Justice and Prosperity, for example, walking hand in hand to convey the official view of the host country. It is recorded that Queen Elizabeth the First was met on one of her official visits by a number of females who were removing blocks from the road, supposedly placed there by the person of Envy: a pleasant piece of allegorical flattery. Again, a stage mime can be allegorical. In Samuel Beckett's mime, *Act Without Words*, a single human actor is repeatedly flung backwards on the stage by unseen agents. In a desert beneath a hot sun, a tree and a

1

carafe of water appear before him, but as he tries to avail of their benefits they disappear. The actor continues to struggle against his invisible tormentors, but in the end he falls, and as the curtain descends, he is lying on the stage, staring helplessly before him. All of this can be taken as an allegorical comment on the human lot.

When we come to examine literary allegory, we discover that an entire work may be allegorical, or that a work may contain one or more allegorical episodes. Milton's *Comus* is a fully-developed moral allegory. Other fully allegorical works are Spenser's *Faerie Queene* Bunyan's *Pilgrim's Progress,* Dryden's *Absalom and Achitophel* and Orwell's *Animal Farm.* Incidental allegory is found in Shakespeare's *Coriolanus*, and in Book Two of Milton's *Paradise Lost.* The first book of Swift's *Guilliver's Travels* is a political allegory; his *Tale of a Tub* is a mainly religious allegory. The allegorical part of *Coriolanus* is the Fable of the Belly (I, i, 97 ff). Menenius tells the mutinous citizens a story:

> There was a time when all the body's members
> Rebelled agaist the Belly; thus accused it
> That only like a gulf it did remain
> In the midst of the body, idle and unactive . . . .

Having developed his fable at some length, he then interprets the underlying allegory :

> The Senators of Rome are this good Belly
> And you the mutinous members . . .

The allegory of Sin (650ff) and Death (666ff) in Book Two of *Paradise Lost* is based on the biblical text : 'When lust was conceived, it bringeth forth sin, and sin, when it is finished, bringeth forth death' (James, 1, 15). Sin is half a female figure, half a serpent, armed with a mortal sting; death is a misshapen male creature, the son of Satan by sin. Allegory came much more naturally to Renaissance writers than it does to modern ones. The almost universal Renaissance view of the universe in terms of various levels of correspondences encouraged the tendency to discover relationships in every direction, and to express one thing in terms of another, thereby cultivating all forms of allegory.

An essential feature of allegory is that it is to be interpreted point by point. Every feature must represent something else. Allegory has been aptly compared to a description in code, always prompting the reader to ask what the persons or articles or events in the story stand for. Another point is that provided each detail in the story stands for something, it is not essential that the persons or events in the allegory should operate according to the laws of probability or even of possibility. Many of the elements in allegorical narrative belong to the world of dreams, where probability matters little; many allegories are, in fact, presented as dreams. Bunyan calls his *Pilgrim's Progress* a work 'in the similitude of a dream', and begins as follows : 'As I walked through the wilderness of this world, I lighted on a certain place where there was a Den, and I laid me down in that place to sleep; and as I slept, I dreamed a dream'. Another dream-like work illustrates the difficulty of trying to classify literary works in formal terms. Austin Clarke's poem, *The Lost Heifer* fulfills one of the main requirements of allegory, since it describes one subject under the guise of another one. *The Lost Heifer* of the title is one of the conventional Gaelic names for Ireland. The poem was written during the Irish Civil War of the nineteen twenties, when the once happy vision of Ireland seemed lost in the prevailing bitterness. But another feature of allegory is missing from the poem: point by point identification of the meaning of some of the details hardly seems possible. The appeal is to the imagination and the feelings rather than to the intellect, and the poem is to this extent symbolist rather than allegorical. (See the article on Symbolism).

The absence of realistic interest in much allegory is illustrated in one of the most famous of all biblical allegories, the story of Pharaoh's dream and its interpretation by Joseph: "So Pharaoh told Joseph, 'In my dream I was standing on the bank of the Nile. And there were seven cows, fat and sleek, coming up out of the Nile, and they began to feed among the rushes. And seven other cows came up after them, starved, ugly and lean: I had never seen such poor cows in all the land of Egypt.

'The lean and ugly cows ate up the seven fat cows. But when they had eaten them up, it was impossible to tell they had eaten them, for they remained as lean as before. Then I woke up. And then again in my dream, there, growing on one stalk, were seven ears of corn, beautifully ripe; but sprouting up after them came seven ears of corn, withered, meagre and scorched by the east wind. The shrivelled ears of corn swallowed the seven ripe ears of corn. I told the magicians this, but no one would tell me the meaning'. Joseph told Pharoah, 'Pharaoh's dreams are one and the same: God has revealed to Pharaoh what he is going to do. The seven fine cows are seven years and the seven ripe ears of corn are seven years; it is one and the same dream. The seven gaunt and lean cows coming up after them are seven years, As are the seven shrivelled ears of corn scorched by the east wind: there will be seven years of famine . . .' (*Genesis* 41).

Pharaoh's dream, and Joseph's point by point interpretation of it, are perfect models of allegory and allegorical commentary. In some allegorical works, such explicit commentary is not provided. Swift, for example, in the first book of *Gulliver's Travels,* does not provide so convenient a key to his underlying meanings, nor does Dryden in *Absalom and Achitophel.* The reader must do this for himself (in modern times with the aid of commentators). It is an interesting fact (and one we can easily overlook) that all commentary on a literary work is a form of allegory to the extent that the commentator presumably thinks that he is disclosing a hidden or not clearly discoverable meaning lurking beneath the surface meaning and needing to be exposed to our view. Myth is another form of allegory. Myths are formulated to explain why our world is as it is, why things happen as they do, why people behave as they do. All myths can be read at more than one level, having meanings to convey in addition to the surface ones.

In a literary work, the entire narrative can be allegorical, which means that the characters are also allegorical. The most elementary example is the beast fable, where the talking animals and their activities are presented for the sake of their parallels with human beings. In some works where the total scheme is not allegorical, characters may function allegorically, or betray the influence of allegory. In *Lycidas,* the allegorical shepherds stand for priests and poets. In Fielding's *Tom Jones,* Squire Allworthy, as his name suggests, is more than a character: he is at least a semi-allegorical figure in a pattern of moral oppositions involving individuals who are far from worthy. Again, the plot of Ben Jonson's *Volpone* is derived from the beast fable, a notable form of allegory. A fable is a short story designed to inculcate a moral about some aspect of human behaviour. Sometimes the moral or lesson is implicit in the fable, sometimes it is explicitly stated in brief form at the end. Most fables (the classic examples are those of Aesop and La Fontaine) employ beasts and birds to represent the deeds and motives of human beings. Most of the chief characters of fable are conventionally presented and motivated (the fox, for example, is almost always sly and malicious) and the same themes tend to recur (punishment for greed, vanity, meddling, and so on). Jonson's Volpone (the fox) is a clever imposter, like many another fox of the beast fable; he exploits the greed of such characters as the lawyer Voltore (the vulture), the miser Corbaccio (the crow), and the merchant Corvino (the raven), Volpone pretends to be dead, and as the rapacious creatures gather round, each expects to own his wealth. Like many of the foxes of fable, Volpone is tricked in the end.

Discussion of allegory inevitably involves some mention of parable. Parable is familiar to every reader of the Gospels, being the means used by Christ to teach. Here is a parable : 'The Kingdom of Heaven is like a merchant in search of fine pearls, who, on finding one pearl of great value, went and sold all that he had and bought it' (Matthew XIII, 45-6). Many writers would claim that every parable is an allegory and that every allegory is a parable. But usage suggests that parable is a more appropriate name for a short illustrative story designed to answer a single question or to point one definite moral, while allegory is preferred when the story is of greater length, not necessarily restricted to one single idea, and less concerned to teach. The object of a parable is to persuade or to teach; not all allegories have this object. Some allegories are written primarily to entertain, or to expose what the writer sees as a deplorable situation, or to hold enemies up to ridicule. In the case of parable, the didactic function is paramount. A lesson or doctrine is to be taught. Direct expression may well prove ineffective, so the parable is tried and conveys the idea in a direct, concrete, easily assimilated fashion. Another point to be made about the distinction between parable and allegory is that in the former, the figures are always what they profess to be and behave according to type. The persons and events do not stand, one by one, for anybody or anything else. The merchant in the parable quoted above is simply a merchant, for example. And gospel parables do not feature lean cows eating fat cows, or shrivelled ears of corn swallowing ripe ones, as does the allegorical dream of Pharaoh. However, there are cases where the gospel parables have all the features of a brief allegory. The parable of the vineyard, for example (Matthew, XXI, 33–41) is an allegory of God's dealings with His people. Each of the details of the story, in true allegorical fashion, represents something else. In the New Testament we often find allegorical meaning attributed to events described in the Old. For example : 'As Jonas was three days and three nights in the whale's belly, so shall the Son of Man be three days and three nights in the heart of the earth' (Matthew XII, 40–20). Jonas in the whale's belly is seen here as an allegory of Christ's descent into hell and His resurrection.

The following brief comments on some classic English allegorical works may help to illustrate the nature of allegory.

(a) Spenser's *Faerie Queene* (1590–1596). This is a continuous allegory, all the details of which may be taken at more than one level of meaning. Take, for example, the description of the Palace of Pride in Book I, Canto IV. On the surface we are concerned with architecture; beneath the surface we are expected to recognize moral implications:

> A stately Palace built of squared brick
> Which cunningly was without mortar laid
> Whose walls were high, but nothing strong, nor thick,
> And golden foile all over them displaid,
> The purest sky with brightness they dismaid;
> High lifted up were many lofty towers,
> And goodly galleries far over laid,
> Full of fair windows and delightful bowers;
> And on the top a Diall told the timely hours.

This fine piece of descriptive writing may be enjoyed for its own sake, but its purpose goes beyond simple enjoyment. We are to recognize that each detail of the great structure represents an aspect of pride, and that the basic features of the palace are also essential features of pride: surface attractiveness going along with underlying instability. The last line hints at the eventual fall of the building.

(b) Bunyan's *Pilgrim's Progress* (1678). This is an allegorical representation of the individual Christian's struggle to achieve salvation, as well as an allegory of all the major Christian doctrines as Bunyan understood them. The Pilgrim of the title is called Christian; he flees the City of Destruction on the advice of Evangelist and makes for the Celestial City through a series of dangerous adventures, encountering temptations (the Giant Despair, Vanity Fair and so on), but eventually reaching his goal. At all points in Bunyan's narrative, the allegorical meaning is clear, at least to the reader familiar with the Bible.

(c) Dryden's *Absalom and Achitophel* (1681). This poem is a splendid allegory of the political situation in England in the early 1680's. Charles the Second, supported by the Tory party, wanted his Catholic brother James the Second to succeed him to the throne. The Whigs, led by the Earl of Shaftesbury, hoped to exclude James in favour of Monmouth, the King's illegitimate son. After Shaftesbury had been charged with High Treason in 1681, the Tories asked Dryden to write a poem on the issues involved to counteract Tory propaganda. He found a remarkably good parallel to the English situation in the biblical story of David, Absalom and Achitophel. The biblical Achitophel encouraged the rebellion of Absalom against his father, King David. Dryden's English Achitophel (Shaftesbury) had a similar influence on Monmouth (Dryden's Absalom). The wrongs suffered by the biblical David could be closely paralleled in those of Charles the Second, as could his uxoriousness. These and other striking parallels between late seventeenth century English politics and one of the best political narratives of the Old Testament (*II Kings,* xv–xvii) help to make Dryden's allegory particularly successful.

(d) Swift's *Gulliver's Travels* (1726). Book One is a close allegory of political conditions and events in the England of the last years of Queen Anne and the first of George the First. The allegory is well disguised. English party politics are presented as an absurd struggle between two groups whose main difference is that one wears high heels and the other favours slightly lower ones; the animosities between the two parties run so high 'that they will neither eat nor drink nor talk with each other'. Again, violent differences arise over the proper way to break eggs before eating them, with the result that many of those who refused to break them at the smaller end have been put to death. The High Heel and the Low Heel parties are the Tories and Whigs; religious controversies are presented in terms of differences over egg-breaking. Allegorical episodes occur frequently in the other books of *Gulliver's Travels*. In Book Three, Laputa, the flying island, is the Court and government of George the First. The Laputans cannot crush the revolt of Lindalino (Dublin), because they are afraid of the combustible fuel directed by the rebels at the island's bottom: an allegory of Swift's own *Drapier's Letters*, by means of which he had won a major victory over the English administration.

(e) Orwell's *Animal Farm* (1945). The idea of this allegorical satire was derived from Book Four of Gulliver's Travels, which is also based on a fable featuring talking animals. Orwell's satire is an explicit allegory of the Russian revolution and the rise of Stalin. The parallels are easily traced. Napoleon is Stalin, and Snowball is Trotsky, whose quarrel with Stalin after Lenin's death led to his expulsion from the Communist party and from Russia. Molly represents those Russians who fled the country after 1917. Boxer is an image of the loyal, uncomplaining proletariat, Moses an unattractive version of the Russian Orthodox Church, while the Battle of the Windmill stands for the German invasion of 1941. While it is true that such parallels can be traced with the utmost precision, the book will survive because in it Orwell embodies universal political truths: what he describes is what happens, sooner or later, to all revolutionary movements.

There are various theoretical objections to allegory as a literary form. Even the most sophisticated allegory presupposes a separation between the idea and the objects through which it is expressed. The 'mechanical' nature of the parallels and their development, the appeal of allegory to the intellect and to knowledge rather than to the imagination and the instinctive feelings, are common sources of discontent, as is the fact that the writer of allegory starts off with his truth, his abstract idea, which his fable is then framed to illustrate. Again, allegory can leave itself open to didactic exploitation, to propaganda and to preaching, thereby almost inevitably falling short of the highest standards of artistic achievement. Blake's pronouncement on the subject expresses a common attitude. He distinguishes between fable or allegory and what he calls 'Vision' (the modern equivalent of which is symbolism). 'Fable or allegory', he declares, 'are a totally distinct and inferior kind of poetry'; the inferiority residing in the fact that symbols have a depth of meaning and significance which can only be dimly suggested by abstract explanations, whereas the meaning of allegory can all too easily be encompassed by these means.

See separate article on Symbolism.

Bibliography: C. S. Lewis, *The Allegory of Love*, 1936, Oxford University Press; N. Frye, *Anatomy of Criticism*, 1957, Oxford University Press; Edwin Honig, *Dark Conceit: The Making of Allegory*, 1959, Faber; G. Hough, *A Preface to the Faerie Queen*, 1962, Duckworth; Angus Fletcher, *Allegory: The Theory of a Symbolic Mode*, 1964, Cornell University Press; R. M. Tuve, *Allegorical Imagery*, Princeton, New Jersey, 1966, Princeton University Press; J. McQueen, *Allegory*, 1970, Methuen; P. Bayley, *Edmund Spenser: Prince of Poets*, 1971, Hutchinson.

Ambiguity

As defined in Webster's Dictionary, ambiguity means 'doubtfulness or uncertainty, particularly as to the signification of language, arising from its admitting of more than one meaning – an equivocal word or expression'. Ambiguous words, phrases, sentences, then, are those capable of being understood in either of two or more possible senses. Traditionally, 'ambiguity' and 'ambiguous' have been used as terms of censure, as in Milton's 'What have been thy answers? what but dark / Ambiguous and with double sense deluding?' In modern critical idiom, the terms retain their original meanings, but instead of being applied unfavourably, tend to be seen as descriptive of qualities which distinguish poetry from other forms of discourse.

The widespread currency of the term 'ambiguity' may be traced to William Empson's celebrated *Seven Types of Ambiguity* (first published 1930; second edition, 1961). Empson's definition of the term is as follows: 'An ambiguity, in ordinary speech, means something very pronounced, and as a rule witty or deceitful. I propose to use the word in an extended sense, and shall think relevant to my subject any verbal nuance, however slight, which gives room for alternative reactions to the same piece of language' (1961 edn., p. 1). To illustrate his use of the term, Empson chose a line from Shakespeare's Sonnet 73:

Bare ruin'd choirs, where late the sweet birds sang

and found this effective in several ways at once. His explanation of its multiple effectiveness, its rich diversity of suggestion for him, is worth quoting to illustrate how much significance the critical method he based on 'ambiguity' as a feature of poetry can extract from even a single line. The comparison, Empson suggests, between monastery choirs and the bare trees holds good for many reasons: 'because ruined monastery choirs are places in which to sing, because they involve sitting in a row, because they are made of wood, are carved into knots and so forth, because they used to be surrounded by a sheltering building crystallised out of the likeness of a forest and coloured like stained glass and painting like flowers and leaves, because they are now abandoned by all but the grey walls coloured like the skies of winter, because the cold and narcissistic charm suggested by the choir-boys suits well with Shakespeare's feeling for the object of the sonnets, and for various sociological and historical reasons . . . . these reasons, and many more relating the simile to its place in the sonnet, must all combine to give the line its beauty, and there is a sort of ambiguity in not knowing which of them to hold most clearly in the mind. Clearly this is involved in all such richness and heightening of effect, and the machinations of ambiguity are among the very roots of poetry' (*Seven Types*, pp. 2–3).

The brilliant success of Empson's sometimes eccentric explorations of several works prompted a generation of disciples in the 'forties and 'fifties to undertake the minute analysis (mainly of shorter poems, for obvious reasons) with a view to exposing each verbal nuance and such associated features as irony and paradox. What could be done with almost any poem using Empson's methods is easily illustrated. Consider the opening line of Keats's *Ode on a Grecian Urn*:

Thou still unravished bride of quietness

As the line stands in the best editions, it contains an ambiguity: the urn is still intact; it is also still *and* intact. A comma after 'still' would turn the word into an adjective and destroy the ambiguity. The work of Marvell, as Empson himself demonstrated, was a rich field for the gleaner of ambiguities. His discovery of multiple meanings in many lines of such poems as *The Garden* (in his *Some Versions of Pastoral*, 1935) and in some poems of Donne and Herbert (in *Seven Types*) enlarged the interest of these works, while still provoking sometimes dismissive rejoinders from specialists.

The discovery of ambiguities can sometimes be a matter of recognizing the vital influence of punctuation on meaning. It was, indeed, by playing with unpunctuated versions of lines in a Shakespearian sonnet that Robert Graves and Laura Riding evolved the critical method which inspired Empson's *Seven Types*. The varied possibilities inherent in this procedure are clear if one examines these lines from Milton describing Adam's response to Paradise:

> all things sɪniled,
> With fragrance and with joy my heart o'erflow'd
> (*Paradise Lost,* Book VIII, 265–6)

A movement of the comma to various other positions causes the sense of the lines to vary minutely but perceptibly (e.g. 'All things smiled with fragrance, / And with joy my heart o'erflow'd'; 'All things smiled with fragrance and with joy, / My heart o'erflow'd', and so on).

Some poets and kinds of poetry are richer in ambiguous implication than others. There are cases, as, for example, Marvell's *Horatian Ode on Cromwell's Return from Ireland,* where ambiguity is the defining characteristic of a poem. Denis Davison's comment is appropriate: 'Many words and phrases in this poem seem to be deliberately ambiguous (and in some cases we cannot be sure whether Marvell is being sarcastic or serious) and this adds a tentative quality to the argument which mirrors Marvell's reservations and doubts as he discusses with himself the complex choice with which history is facing him . . . . Marvell's Ode is permeated by ambiguities — ambiguities which do not confuse but which ask us to consider carefully the alternative interpretations of the complex historical problem. Thus "restless Cromwell" implies both admiration for his untiring activity and a warning that his inherent dynamism may have to be curbed. Similarly, the soldiers who applaud the execution of Charles with 'bloody hands' are viewed both as men who have ventured their lives for their cause and as men guilty of the blood of Charles' (*Marvell: Poems,* 1964, p. 46).

Marvell's poem, then, invites discussion in terms of Empson's method. So, too, does a poem like Hopkins' *The Windhover,* every line of which has yielded up a rich store of multiple meanings to patient and intensive investigation:

> I caught this morning morning's minion, Kingdom of
> daylight's dauphin, dapple-dawn-drawn Falcon, in his riding
> Of the rolling level underneath him steady air, and striding
> High there, how he rung upon the rein of a wimpling wing. . .

Most commentators point to two possible interpretations of 'dapple-dawn-drawn Falcon'. The bird may be drawn (etched, outlined) against the dappled dawn or drawn upwards into the dawn. 'How he rung upon the rein' has provoked many plausible interpretations. One commentator feels that 'rung' calls to mind the ringing bells with which the reins are adorned as befitting a royal charger, and that 'rein' is a homophone of 'reign', recalling the fact that the hawk is a dauphin, a prince. But another suggests that 'to ring upon the rein' is a metaphor from horse-training,the sweeping curves of the bird's flight being seen in terms of the circle described by a horse at the end of a trainer's long rein. But 'to ring' is also a technical term from falconry, meaning to rise in spirals. Then again, it has been suggested that the image is really that of the falcon, bell-like, swinging back and forth.

Many ambiguities are, of course, puns (for example 'rein/reign' above), but Empson did not want to describe all puns as ambiguities. 'If a pun is quite obvious', he suggested, 'it would not ordinarily be called ambiguous, because there is no room for puzzling'. He would, however, call it ambiguous when 'we recognize that there could be a puzzle as to what the author meant, in that alternative views might be taken without sheer misreading' (*Seven Types*, p. x). Pope's famous lines

> Where Bentley late tempestuous wont to sport
> In troubled waters, but now sleeps in port
> (*The Dunciad*, Book IV, 201–2)

contain a clever pun suggestive of Bentley's controversial temperament and his weakness for liquor, but are not really ambiguous. A slightly less clear case is that presented by the following:

> To happy Convents, bosom'd deep in vines,
> Where slumber Abbots, purple as their wines
> (*The Dunciad*, Book IV, 301–2)

Most readers would probably feel that the bibulousness of the abbots is clearly enough suggested here to preclude genuine ambiguity. The latter, however, is present in Marvell's lines about Charles I on the scaffold:

> He nothing common did or mean
> Upon that memorable scene;
> But with his keener eye
> The Axe's edge did try

(Horatian Ode)

The ambiguity of the last two lines resides in the fact that Marvell is probably remembering the Latin *acies* (eyesight *and* sharp edge).

As to the value of 'ambiguity' as a critical term and of verbal analysis as a technique, opinions vary. T. S. Eliot held them in low esteem. 'The method', he wrote, 'is to take a well-known poem . . . without reference to the author or to his other work, to analyse it stanza by stanza and line by line, and extract, squeeze, tease, press every drop of meaning out of it that one can' (*On Poetry and Poets*, 1957, p. 113). Eliot christened it 'the lemon-squeezer school of criticism'. But its practitioners would argue that the ambiguities they reveal are poetic facts, and that it is a characteristic of poetry to suggest more than it says. On the other hand, it is going too far to suggest that poetic discourse is distinguished from other kinds by the presence of paradox and ambiguity. J. M. Cameron's comment on this notion is admirably sane: 'Certainly, paradox and ambiguity can be identified in much of the poetry that moves us deeply, and the critic can show that the power of such poetry to move us is connected with the successful employment of these devices. But paradox and ambiguity could only be the essentially distinguishing marks of poetry if we did not have a use for paradox and ambiguity in other forms of discourse. This is plainly false' (*The Night Battle*, 1962, p. 134).

The technique of verbal analysis can obviously be abused by critics determined to find multiple meanings everywhere. Even the best verbal critics are sometimes guilty of over-reading, particularly when they ignore the limitations placed upon their method by literary and historical context. This is what John Press has in mind when he writes of Marvell's poetry, with critics like Empson in mind, that 'some of the recent scholarship and critical ingenuity lavished upon his poems appears to be misplaced for, while it is undeniable that he was a highly subtle writer, certain critics have attributed to him philosophical implications and verbal ambiguities of which he himself was unaware' (*Andrew Marvell*, 1958, p. 14). T. S. Eliot, writing about a book called *Interpretations*, in which critics closely analysed twelve poems, including one of his own, suggested that 'to study twelve poems each analysed so painstakingly is a very tiring way of passing the time. I imagine that some of the poets (they are all dead except myself) would be surprised at learning what their poems mean. I had one or two minor surprises myself' (*On Poetry and Poets*, p. 113). However, there is a sense in which the multiple meanings suggested by an Empson (whether historically validated or not) become part of the meanings of the poems in question, just as the meanings accumulated by Shakespeare's plays over three and a half centuries (the result of the insights of critics of genius) cannot be disregarded merely because they are not susceptible of certain demonstration, or even because they are 'unhistorical'.

Bibliography: W. Empson, *Seven Types of Ambiguity*, 1930, Chatto; *Some Versions of Pastoral*, 1935, Chatto; R. Graves and L. Riding, eds. *A Survey of Modernist Poetry*, 1938; C. Brooks and R. P. Warren, eds. *Understanding Poetry*, 1938, Holt; C. Brooks, *The Well Wrought Urn*, 1947, Harcourt Brace; P. Wheelright, *The Burning Fountain*, 1954, Indiana University Press; L. D. Lerner, *Chapter on Marvell's Horation Ode* in '*Interpretations*', ed. J. Wain, 1955, Routledge; C. Ricks, *Milton's Grand Style*, 1963, Oxford University Press; John Wain, *Interpretations*, 1955, Routledge; S. Fish, *Surprised by Sin*, 1967, Macmillan; J. B. Leishman, *The Art of Marvell's Poetry*, 1968, Hutchinson.

The Ballad

It is easier to describe the ballad than to define it. Most writers on the form distinguish three kinds of ballad: the traditional, the literary and the popular. Traditional ballad or folk ballad is a name given to a type of verse of unknown authorship, dealing with a single episode or simple motif rather than with a sustained theme. It is a song, transmitted orally, commenting on life by telling a story in a popular style. Successive singers who sang the traditional ballads learned them by word of mouth, and tended to introduce changes, with the result that such ballads exist in numerous variant forms. Here are two versions of the first stanza of *The Unquiet Grave:*

> Cold blows the wind to my true love,
>   And gently drops the rain,
> I never had but one sweetheart,
>   And in greenwood she lies slain,
>   And in greenwood she lies slain.

> The wind doth blow to-day, my love,
> And a few small drops of rain;
> I never had but one true love,
> In cold grave she was lain.

The basic requirement of the traditional ballad is that it should be suitable for transmission in oral form. This naturally had a major influence in determining its main features. Traditional ballads tend to be comparatively short, simple in plot and in metrical structure. In an essay on Kipling, a twentieth-century master of the ballad form, T. S. Eliot puts the matter well: 'The attention of the reader is concentrated on the story and the characters; and a ballad must have a meaning immediately apprehensible by its auditors. Repeated hearings may confirm the first impressions, may repeat the effect, but full understanding should be conveyed at one hearing. The metrical form must be of a simple kind which will not call attention to itself, but repetitions and refrains may contribute an incantatory effect. There should be no metrical complications corresponding to subtleties of feeling that cannot be immediately responded to'. (*On Poetry and Poets,* 1957, p. 231). Eliot's remarks apply to every kind of ballad.

Since the ballad is essentially a narrative, and not a lyrical, exercise, it is impersonal in character. The narrator does not intervene in his own person, express personal attitudes or feelings, or make explicit judgments on his characters. Psychological analysis is not a feature of the ballad. Ballads are fundamentally dramatic in style; ballad language is a language of action and event, not of reflection or analysis. The story is told in flashes, and each stanza embodies a separate passage of dialogue or a distinct scene. There are sudden narrative shots, vivid dreamlike images; pictures are juxtaposed. The narrator generally begins with a climactic episode, and tells his story tersely and economically by means of action and dialogue. Sometimes (as in Auden's 'O what is that sound') he achieves his story-telling purpose by means of dramatic dialogue alone. The first two stanzas of the greatest of all ballads, *Sir Patrick Spens,* exemplify the main features of the balladeer's method:

> The king sits in Dumferling toune,
>   Drinking the blude-reid wine:
> 'O whar will I get guid sailor,
>   To sail this schip of mine?'
>
> Up and spak an eldern knicht,
>   Sat at the kings richt kne:
> 'Sir Patrick Spence is the best sailor
>   That sails upon the sea'.

Here we have the conventionally abrupt and arresting opening, the brief, economical sketch of the setting and action, the sharp transition from narrative to dialogue and back again. The same features may be studied in the opening stanzas of Coleridge's *Ancient Mariner,* which is a literary ballad (for the distinction between the traditional and the literary ballad see below). Coleridge's curt, businesslike transition from scene-setting to narrative is particularly noteworthy. *Sir Patrick Spens,* incidentally, poses a nice problem of classification. One might be forgiven for thinking it a fine example of the traditional ballad. In his *Reliques of Ancient English Poetry* (1765) Bishop Percy describes it as having been transmitted from Scotland, but there is no indication that it comes from folk tradition, nor can a historical basis be found for the events it relates. Like many antique-looking ballads, it may, in fact, be a purely literary composition of the eighteenth century. (See M. J. C. Hodgart's remarks in his Introduction to the *Faber Book of Ballads*, 1965, p. 17).

The traditional ballad is a highly stylised, conventional form. Typical features, apart from the swift transitions and economical presentation, include refrains and repetitions and, very often, a strong sense of ironic inevitability (Scott's *Rosabelle*, for example, a sophisticated version of the traditional ballad). In many traditional ballads we find stock descriptive phrases ('milk-white steed'; 'blood-red wine') and clichés of numbers (three being the most popular) as well as the device known as 'incremental repetition', in which a line or stanza is repeated but with some addition which advances the story. There is also a conventional ballad stanza form. The normal stanza has four lines, with alternate four and three foot lines, rhyming ABCB (or occasionally, as in some stanzas of *The Ancient Mariner*, ABCBDB).

The second kind, the literary ballad, is a narrative poem written by a learned poet (the traditional ballad was the product of a pre-literate community) in conscious and sophisticated imitation of the form and spirit of the traditional ballad. Many of the remarks made above on the conventional features of the traditional ballad are therefore applicable to the literary ballad as well. Some of the greatest English literary ballads belong to the Romantic period: Coleridge's *Ancient Mariner* (much longer and more elaborate than any traditional ballad; Keats's *La Belle Dame Sans Merci;* Scott's *Proud Maisie.* Romantic writers looked nostalgically to the past in their quest for a simpler, more 'natural' way of life than they saw around them. They found this best expressed in traditional ballads. Bishop Percy's collection of folk-songs and ballads, *Reliques of Ancient English Poetry* (1765), gave a powerful impetus to composition in the form.

All the great Romantic poets were influenced to some degree by the traditional ballad. Coleridge's *Ancient Mariner* traces a significant part of its descent from *Sir Patrick Spens* and other ballads in Percy's *Reliques*. George Watson (in *Coleridge the Poet*, 1966, p. 87) has pointed out that *The Ancient Mariner* is almost the only poem in the first edition of *Lyrical Ballads* which is a ballad in the precise historical sense, almost the only one using the ballad-metre that Percy's collection had made familiar to educated readers since 1765 (alternating four and three-foot lines, rhyming ABCB or sometimes ABCBDB). Only two poems by Wordsworth in the collection are strictly in ballad-metre: *We are Seven* and *The Tables Turned*. Another great Romantic literary ballad, Keats's *La Belle Dame Sans Merci*, represents a variation on the traditional ballad stanza, the final line of each stanza having four syllables, not six (two strong beats, not four), which makes for an appropriately solemn emphasis. Keats's narrative belongs to a widely popular folk legend whose best-known literary version was a mediaeval ballad called *Thomas Rymer*, which Keats found in Jamieson's *Popular Ballads* (1806).

A third kind of ballad is the popular ballad. Whereas the traditional ballad took its rise in a pre-literate rural community, the popular ballad is the product of a literate or at least semi-literate urban population. The values of the traditional ballad are heroic; those of the popular ballad are realistic and unheroic. The traditional ballad is usually tragic in tone, while the popular ballad tends towards comedy. The traditional ballad is a dignified exercise, the popular ballad a comparatively 'undignified' one. Much traditional balladry is aristocratic in its attitudes; the popular ballad is the poetry of the common man. It is, by contrast, uncourtly, unsentimental and irreverent. The popular ballad, also frequently called the broadside ballad, or street ballad, because it was printed on a single broadsheet and hawked about the streets, deals with a current event or issue in racy, homely language. Some important English poets, among them Pope, Swift and Byron, were masters of the popular ballad. Reference has already been made to the influence of the traditional ballad on writers of literary ballads. The popular ballad also influenced many English poets. This influence may be traced in Shakespeare's plays (Hamlet and Ophelia are familiar with a wide range of street ballads, for example). It is, however, in the work of the Romantics that the street ballad exerts its greatest power. A

number of *Blake's Songs of Innocence and Experience* have been
well described as street ballads transfigured and spiritualised.
Wordsworth was strongly influenced by street ballads in his
contribution to *Lyrical Ballads* (1798), a volume which con-
tained Coleridge's *Ancient Mariner* and, oddly enough in view
of the title, *Tintern Abbey* as well. Wordsworth's ballads are
mainly imitations of the popular, broadsheet ballads of the
eighteenth century. Robert Burns wrote a sequence of ballads
called *The Jolly Beggars,* which preserve the rhythm, style and
tone of the old street ballads. In *The Cloud,* Shelley used the
street-ballad stanza, while his most famous 'popular' poem,
The Masque of Anarchy, preserves the idiom and form of the
street ballad. Yeats was to transform the Dublin street-ballad
in such poems as *Sixteen Dead Men* and *The Rose Tree,* while for
his best-known poem, *The Ballad of Reading Gaol,* Wilde was
indebted to the same popular tradition.

The ballad, whether traditional, literary or popular, is
capable of accommodating a wide variety of effects. In his account of Keats's *La Belle Dame Sans Merci,* Earl Wasserman
points out that 'it would be difficult in any reading of Keats's
ballad not to be enthralled by the haunting power of its
rhythm, by its delicate intermingling of the fragile and the
grotesque, the tender and the weird, and by the perfect
economy by which these effects are achieved' (*The Finer Tone,
Keats's Major Poems,* 1953, p. 65). The same remarks are appropriate to Coleridge's *Ancient Mariner,* with its juxtaposition
of gruesome effects with lyrical passages on the beauty of the
natural world and exotic descriptions of supernatural
phenomena. The greatest ballads are characterised by a sense
of mystery and incompleteness, suggestive overtones (the
background against which the events are set is often only
glanced at or conveyed by means of vague hints), and a frequently ironical, sometimes cruel, humour. Ballad imagery is
often stark. Much of the power of the ballad is the result of its
preference for concrete rather than abstract language, a function of its emphasis on immediate experience and directly
rendered action rather than on reflection or analysis.

Bibliography: *Cambridge History of English Literature*, Vol. II, Chapter XVII; 1932 C.U.P. Volume entitled *'The Period of the French Revolution'*, G. H. Gerould, *The Ballad of Tradition*, 1932, Oxford University Press; M. J. C. Hodgart, *Ballads*, 1950, Hutchinson; T. S. Eliot, *'Rudyard Kipling' in On Poetry and Poets*, 1957, Faber; Francis J. Child, *English and Scottish Popular Ballads*, (reissued in 3 volumes), 1957, Oxford University Press; V. de Sola Pinto and A. E. Rodway, eds., *The Common Muse, An Anthology of Popular British Ballad Poetry*, 1957, Chatto and Windus; D. Buchan, *The Ballad and the Folk*, 1972, Routledge and Keegan Paul; C. Carrington ed., *The Complete Barrack-Room Ballads of Rudyard Kipling*, 1973, Methuen; G. Grigson, ed., *The Penguin Book of Ballads*, 1976, Penguin.

Comedy

The subject of this article is dramatic comedy; comment is confined to works written for the stage. Critical discussion of comedy is slight compared with that of tragedy. Critics of every generation have offered definitions of tragedy, but formal, comprehensive attempts to define the essence of comedy have been rare indeed. It is easier to describe the features common to a wide range of dramatic comedies, and to classify the different kinds of dramatic comedy, than to attempt a definition of the form.

It is perhaps best to begin with an account of some of the permanent characteristics of dramatic comedy. From the classical Greeks to the present day, many of its features have remained unchanged, particularly those related to its plot-structure and its character-types. In the great majority of comedies, a love-interest culminating in marriage dictates the progress of the plot. A young man's desire to marry a young woman (or vice-versa) is thwarted by stern opposition, which is finally overcome by some twist or manipulation of the plot. The obstacles to the hero's or heroine's ambition (parental opposition, lack of money, family feuds, misunderstandings, and so on) form the main action of the comedy, while the comic resolution features their conquest, followed by the festive ritual of marriage.

A basic feature of all comedy is its profoundly social character: comic characters are presented in groups and in a social environment. Traditional comedy tends to affirm the fundamental rightness of society: the norms of society are the moral norms of comedy. Deviations from the standards of society are the chief targets of comedy, and deviant characters are the stock comic character-types, to be isolated and ridiculed at least until their faults have been cured. As such deviations become more extreme and more absolute, they move across the boundary separating comedy from tragedy; comedy cures only relatively minor deviations (meanness, boastfulness, unsociability, for example). A primary aim of comedy is to make sport of all kinds of fools and of human folly and absurdity. On the other hand, the writer of comedy cannot disgrace or expose his victims too much without upsetting the comic balance. This, many people would feel, is what happens in the case of Shylock in Shakespeare's *Merchant of Venice*.

Another feature of comedy (if we exclude satiric comedy) is that its victims tend to be absurd (out of harmony with their societies) rather than evil. The judgment of comedy tends to be against what is ridiculous rather than against what is wicked; it tends, in other words, to be social rather than moral, 'to sport with human follies, not with crimes', as Ben Jonson put it (although his own practice is sometimes different). The stock comic characters generally embody or personify some quality which renders them at least temporarily unfit for life in a well-adjusted society. Many of them are dominated by a single passion or obsession. Thus we have the conventional comic miser, the glutton, the gossip, or the hypochondriac (who can never admit for a moment that he enjoys good health). These comic types, and others (the braggart, for example) recur in the comedy of all ages, and can often be identified by their names: Lady Sneerwell and Sir Benjamin Backbite in Sheridan's *School for Scandal;* Malvolio the puritan misanthrope and Sir Toby Belch the glutton in Shakespeare's *Twelfth Night;* Mrs. Malaprop the gross misuser of language in Sheridan's *Rivals* ('She's as headstrong as an allegory on the banks of the Nile'; I would by no means wish a daughter of mine to be a progeny of learning'); Tony Lumpkin (his name a compound of 'lumpen' and 'bumpkin') in Goldsmith's *She Stoops to Conquer;* Volpone (the fox) in Jonson's comedy of the name, who outwits others and is himself finally outwitted. Whereas tragic plot has the function of revealing character, comic plot has not, since the nature of comic characters is decided in advance; they tend to behave according to type.

Comedy is traditionally less realistic, more artificial than tragedy. In Lamb's words, admittedly involving some exaggeration, comedy has 'no reference to the world that is'. What Lamb is thinking of here are such things as the widespread use of disguise and mistaken identity as comic conventions, which are often used to achieve greater complexity of plot. The main plot of *Twelfth Night,* for example, has been summarized, not unfairly, as follows: 'A girl disguised as a boy loves a man who commissions her to woo a lady whose advances she must check'. The circumstances of comic plots often lead characters into gross misconceptions, misunderstandings and confusions. Another artificial feature of comedy is that its endings tend to be contrived, manipulated by some arbitrary turn of the plot; many comedies feature most unlikely conversions, miraculous transformations, last-minute discoveries, providential accidents and coincidences.

The fundamentally social character of comedy has already been stressed. The comic dramatist may be seen as the representative of the majority, the mouthpiece of a tribal response to those who question the standards and norms of a society. The comic victim may be seen as an alien figure whose behaviour or ideas cast doubt on those codes of practice and belief which the majority of people accept as sane and normal. The price to be paid by the victim for acting contrary to the views of the 'sane' majority is his isolation and exposure to ridicule. Comedy is a conservative art. Shakespeare's *Twelfth Night* will serve as an illustration. The social order in Illyria is a carefully-structured one, with rigid lines of demarcation between the various social classes. It is unthinkable that anybody should try to surmount the social barriers. But this is what Malvolio does, and it is primarily because he aspires to marry a great lady (and seriously believes in the possibility of success) that he is made to appear such a fool.

There are various methods of classifying comedies. One common one is to distinguish between (a) Comedy of Manners (b) Satiric Comedy (c) Romantic Comedy (d) Farce.

(a) Comedy of Manners. This form involves sophisticated characters and a realistic background. Fashionable, polished society is its native element. Its dialogue demands prose which both contributes to the 'realistic' atmosphere and provides a suitable vehicle for the witty exchanges, those displays of verbal dexterity which are its most distinctive feature. The antithesis is its characteristic stylistic device. The comedy of manners is intellectual in its impulse, designed, as George Meredith claimed in his essay *The Idea of Comedy*, to evoke 'intellectual laughter' from an audience which is seldom moved to emotional involvement with the characters, but which regards the comic victims from a standpoint of intellectual superiority. These victims are mainly people who pose a threat to the often arbitrary rules of society: fops who are absurd in their affectations, enemies of wit and pleasure, dull people, jealous husbands. We are not moved to regard these figures with sympathy: they are there mainly to provide opportunities for displays of wit at their own expense. Two of Shakespeare's comedies, *Love's Labours Lost* and *Much Ado About Nothing*, with their sustained wit combats between highly intelligent men and women, and their sophisticated social backgrounds, may be classified as comedies of manners. This form of comedy reached one peak of its development in England after the Restoration of Charles II. Dryden, Etherege, Wycherley, Congreve, Vanburgh, and Farquhar are the seventeenth-century masters of the comedy of manners. The milieu is almost entirely aristocratic and the 'manners' displayed by the characters are not those common to men in general, but the affectations peculiar to a cultured élite, not inherent traits, but qualities acquired by them from their society. For all its brilliance, Restoration comedy has consistently been condemned by moralistic critics for its low moral standards. Its values reflect those of Restoration aristocratic society. Macaulay's comment is representative: 'Morality constantly enters into that world, a sound morality and an unsound morality, the sound morality to be insulted, derided, associated with everything mean and hateful; the unsound morality to be set off to every advantage, an inculcated by all methods, direct and indirect'. An inevitable reaction against the moral standards of Restoration comedy led to the dominance in the early eighteenth century of Sentimental Comedy, morally unexceptionable, intended to provoke 'generous pity', 'pure joy', 'sober and polite mirth' rather than laughter. But Sentimental Comedy itself provoked a reaction, which led to the revival of comedy of manners in the 1770's by Goldsmith and Sheridan. However, while these dramatists preserved the wit of Restoration comedy, they rejected its indecencies. Goldsmith's *Good Natured Man* (1768) and *She*

Stoops to Conquer (1773) and Sheridan's *The Rivals* and *The School for Scandal* (1775 and 1777) are the major comedies of the age. An important nineteenth-century example of comedy of manners is Wilde's *The Importance of Being Earnest* (1895).

(b) Satiric Comedy. The writer of satiric comedy has an end in view beyond mere entertainment. His work implies a fundamental dislike of the attitudes and conventions of society, or at least some of these, and is motivated partly by a concern for reform, partly by a sense of superiority which finds an outlet in bitter derision. The greatest English master of satiric comedy is Ben Jonson. His most memorable characters are parasites, rascals, swindlers and worse, incapable of arousing sympathy, but freely arousing disgust and contempt. The vital principle of satiric comedy is ridicule; the chief characters are bitterly pursued for their follies. It was no part of Jonson's theory of comedy that characters should be likeable or good-natured. Satiric comedy has a strongly ethical bent; the offending characters are so severely chastened for their faults that their fates can be seen as exemplary: one is shown, at any rate, what is to be avoided. As one moralistic critic put it before Jonson's time: 'With the scourge of the lewd, the lewd are feared (discouraged) from evil attempts'. The characters of *Volpone*, Jonson's best-known satiric comedy, are embodiments of animal drives, and the dramatist insists on the unredeemed criminality of their actions. He provides no major focus for the audience's sympathy. It is difficult to enjoy a play when one does not like any of its characters.

(c) Romantic Comedy. The great English writer in this form was Shakespeare. Romantic comedy involves love-affairs, an idealized heroine, often a good deal of disguise, and a happy resolution after many obstacles have been surmounted. For the purposes of this account, Romantic comedy is synonymous with Shakespearian comedy. In all Shakespeare's comedies, a love-interest is predominant, but the other 'romantic' aspect of these plays lies in their idealized settings and characters, their distance from everyday reality, their mythic quality (see particularly *A*

Midsummer Night's Dream). Shakespeare's comic world is one of adventure, the principal adventure being love. Other adventures and misadventures are 'jealousies and ficklenesses, mistaken identities, wrongly reported deaths, separations and reunions, disguises of sex and all the other improbabilities that can be fancied, entangled and at last resolved into whole harmony by some happy turn of events' (Nevill Coghill, 'The Basis of Shakespearian Comedy', *Shakespeare Criticism* 1935–1960, 1963, p. 210).

Whereas the comedy of manners flourishes in a world of wit, Shakespearian comedy presents a world of humour. Wit involves detachment; emotional sympathy is essential for humour. The spirit of the comedy of manners is one of mockery of everything seriously at variance with social norms; Shakespearian comedy is good-humoured and magnanimous. Comedy of manners is concerned with the immediate present; Shakespearian comedy is timeless, mingling thoughts of the past and of the future with those of the present; the idea of death is not excluded. The contrast between the 'realistic' settings of comedy of manners and Shakespeare's choice of locations is extreme. Many of Shakespeare's characters may be recognizably Elizabethan, but he places them in the most incongruous settings. In *A Midsummer Night's Dream*, Bottom the Weaver (an Elizabethan 'rude mechanical') appears along with Theseus Duke of Athens and Oberon King of the Fairies. Allardyce Nichol's comments on the broad contrasts between Shakespearian comedy and comedy of manners are worth quoting: 'The extraordinary complexity of intellect and emotion, the real and the imaginary, reminds us that these comedies pursue a path far more perilous than the comedy of manners. All depends here on the exquisite sense of balance possessed by a tight-rope walker. Death must be introduced, but just so much and no more; timelessness is essential, yet the timing must not be forgotten; placelessness too is essential, but the local habitation and the name also are required; the persons have to be seemingly real, yet they are associated with incredible circumstances, and lack of motivation' (*The Theatre and Dramatic Theory*, 1962, p. 137).

Northrop Frye has pointed out that 'comedy blends insensibly into satire at one extreme and into romance at the other'.

Ben Jonson's satiric comedies and Shakespeare's romantic ones illustrate the two extremes. Whereas Jonson's main characters are almost totally disreputable, there is hardly a single Shakespearian comic character from whom one cannot expect some decent impulse. Shakespeare's comic characters arouse admiration, and excite neither scorn nor contempt. They generally inspire us to be happy *with* them as well as to laugh at them. Falstaff, the most complete of all comic creations, defines his own standing as a comic character in a famous passage, and incidentally provides an important comment on Shakespearian comedy: 'Men of all sorts take pride to gird at me. The brain . . . of man is not able to invent anything that intends to laughter more than I invent or is invented on me. I am not only witty in myself, but the cause that wit is in other men' (*Henry IV*, Pt. II, I, ii, 6ff).

Shakespeare's comedies are essentially different from classical comedy, which includes comedy of manners as well as satiric comedy. Classical comedy implies a society which feels secure in its fundamental values, which feels that it has attained acceptable standards of social well-being: its natural targets are therefore those who offend against established codes of public common sense and fitness. Shakespearian comedy, on the other hand, does not assume that the conditions necessary for man's welfare have been established with certainty. As H. B. Charlton puts it, 'it speculates imaginatively on modes, not of preserving a good already reached, but of enlarging and extending the possibilities of this and other kinds of good. Its heroes or heroines . . . are voyagers in pursuit of a happiness not yet attained, a brave new world wherein man's life may be fuller, his sensations more exquisite and his joys more widespread, more lasting, and so more humane . . . Shakespearian comedy is not finally satiric; it is poetic. It is not conservative; it is creative. The way is that of the imagination rather than that of pure reason. It is an artist's vision, not a critic's exposition' (*Shakespearian Comedy*, 1966 edn., p. 278).

(d) Farce. There are two ways of considering farce as a literary or dramatic kind. The term may be used to describe an entire dramatic work, usually short, intended only to excite laughter. The laughter in question is far from the intellectual kind associated with comedy of manners; it is simple, hearty and coarse. We do not expect brilliant wit-combats in a farce. Farce makes little or no appeal to the intellect or to the higher emotions: it encourages a primitive response to clownish physical and verbal activity. It generally involves crude or boisterous jesting and broad humour, and is marked by little subtlety of dialogue or plot. It naturally presupposes a less discriminating audience than do the higher forms of comedy. The characters of a farce are not presented for their fidelity to nature; they are generally types, caricatures. The farcical dramatist achieves bold effects by placing such characters in odd, improbable and ridiculous situations. A basic difference between pure comedy and farce lies in the degree of their fidelity to nature. Farce exploits unlikely, even unnatural, events and situations for the sake of merriment alone. Pure comedy is concerned with the presentation of character and manners, and invariably has a serious dimension. The laughter of comedy is a measured laughter; the aim of farce is to keep up a continuous roar of merriment.

Few plays are pure farces. We usually encounter farce as an element in a more sophisticated form of comedy. Many famous comedies have farcical episodes or interludes. Classification depends on the comic quality of a play as a whole rather than that of particular parts – even memorable ones. Some comedies present problems in this respect. One is J. M. Synge's *Playboy of the Western World,* the first draft of which is entitled *The Murderer, A Farce.* Successive re-writings modified the farcical character of the original, but large elements of farce remain. Whether these colour the play sufficiently to make it a farce rather than a comedy is debatable. We have, for example, the baiting of Shawn Keogh, the presentation of Old Mahon, the horseplay involving Christy:

Shawn Pull a twist on his neck, and squeeze him so.
Philly Twist yourself. Sure he cannot hurt you, if you keep your distance from his teeth alone.
Shawn I'm afraid of him. (*to Pegeen*) Lift a lighted sod, will you, and scorch his leg.

Pegeen (*blowing the fire with a bellows*) Leave go now, young
          man, or I'll scorch your shins . . . (*Christy squirms round
          on the floor and bites Shawn's leg*)
Shawn (*shrieking*) My leg's bit on me. He's like a mad dog,
          I'm thinking, the way that I will surely die.

(Act III)

The relationship between laughter and comedy is an important topic. In some critical discussions, the two are treated as
synonymous terms. But this attitude does not do full justice to
the complexity of comedy. It is true that certain comedies do
stimulate fairly continuous laughter, which appears to be
their *raison d'être*. One thinks of *The Importance of Being Earnest*,
a play which has all the marks of having been constructed
primarily to provoke repeated laughter. It is possible to isolate
the main device used by Wilde to achieve this effect: the
systematic employment of the remark with its immediate
comic reversal usually coming from someone else:

Lady Bracknell Do you smoke?
Jack Well yes, I must admit I smoke.
Lady Bracknell I am glad to hear it. A man should always
          have an occupation of some kind . . . Are your parents
          living?
Jack I have lost both my parents.
Lady Bracknell To lose one parent, Mr. Worthing, may be
          regarded as a misfortune: to lose both looks like
          carelessness.

It is interesting that Wilde himself called *The Importance* 'a
somewhat farcical comedy', recognizing, perhaps, that pure
comedy, unlike farce, does not depend for its enjoyment on
continuous laughter. Ben Jonson, whose own comedies are
often no laughing matter, observed: 'Nor is the moving of
laughter always the end of comedy'. Bernard Shaw found
fault with Wilde's play because it did little more than cause
successive waves of laughter to engulf the theatre. 'It amused
me, of course', Shaw wrote, 'but unless comedy touches me as
well as amuses me, it leaves me with a sense of having wasted
my evening'. Shaw is here hinting at a profound truth about
comedy. Most people expect to laugh during the performance

of a comedy, but good comedy cannot be summed up in terms of laughter alone. There are many successful comedies which provoke comparatively little laughter, and tragedies which can arouse hysterical laughter. In many Shakespearian comedies, there are comparatively few 'laugh-lines', and the same is true of Shaw's, which suggests that the equation of laughter with comedy need not be taken too seriously.

See separate article on Wit and Humour.

Bibliography: B. Dobreé, *Restoration Comedy,* 1924, Oxford University Press; E. Welsford, *The Fool,* 1935, Faber; H. B. Charlton, *Shakesperian Comedy,* 1938, Methuen; L. J. Potts, *Comedy,* 1949, Hutchinson; W. Sypher, ed., *Comedy* (contains George Meredith's *Essay on Comedy* and Henri Bergson's *Laughter*), Harvard University Press, 1949; A. S. Cook, *The Dark Voyage and the Golden Mean,* Cambridge, Mass., 1949, Harvard University Press; N. Frye, *Anatomy of Criticism,* 1957, Oxford University Press; J. R. Brown, *Shakespeare and His Comedies,* 1957, Metheun; Paul Lauter, ed., *Theories of Comedy,* New York, 1964, Doubleday; R. W. Corrigan, *Comedy: Meaning and Form,* San Francisco, 1965, Chandler Publishing Company; E. Olson, *The Theory of Comedy,* 1968, Indiana University Press; M. Esslin, *The Theatre of the Absurd,* 1968, Penguin; J. L. Styan, *The Dark Comedy,* 1968, Cambridge University Press; J. B. Bamborough, *Ben Jonson,* 1970, Hutchinson; K. Muir, *The Comedy of Manners,* 1970, Hutchinson; A. C. Dessen, *Jonson's Moral Comedy,* 1971, Northwestern University Press; M. Merchant, *Comedy,* 1972, Methuen; M. Bradbury and D. Palmer, eds., *Shakespearian Comedy,* Stratford-upon-Avon Studies, 14, 1972, E. Arnold.

Conceit

The term 'conceit' is generally used for figures of speech which establish arresting parallels between objects which at first glance seem to have little or nothing in common. Helen Gardner's description is worth quoting: 'A conceit is a comparison whose ingenuity is more striking than its justness, or at least is more immediately striking. All comparisons discover likeness in things unlike: a comparison becomes a conceit when we are made to concede likeness while being strongly conscious of unlikeness. A brief comparison can be a conceit if two things patently unlike, or which we should never think of together, are shown to be alike in a single point in such a way, or in such a context, that we feel their incongruity' (*The Metaphysical Poets*, 1957, Introduction, p. 19). The conceit is the favourite and characteristic device of the seventeenth-century Metaphysical poets, and the most famous remarks on its use are those of Samuel Johnson in his essay on one of these poets, Abraham Cowley. Johnson saw the conceit as a figure whereby poets could (often misguidedly, in his view) display their wit, which he described as 'a kind of *discordia concors*: a combination of dissimilar images, or discovery of occult resemblances in things apparently unlike. Of wit thus defined, they (the Metaphysical poets) have more than enough . . . The most heterogeneous ideas are yoked by violence together; nature and art are ransacked for illustrations, comparisons and allusions; their learning instructs, and their subtlety surprises, but the reader commonly thinks his improvement dearly bought' (*Life of Cowley*).

Few twentieth-century critics would accept Johnson's strictures on the Metaphysical conceit. Some examples are, admittedly, tasteless, tactless and over-ingenious, as the following from Crashaw's *Weeper*, a poem about Mary Magdalen:

> Upwards dost thou weep;
> Heaven's bosom drinks the gentle stream;
> Where the milky rivers creep
> Thine floats above and is the cream

A much better conceit on the same topic is found in Marvell's
Eyes and Tears:

> So Magdalen with tears more wise
> Dissolved those captivating eyes,
> Whose liquid chains could flowing meet
> To fetter her Redeemer's feet.

The best Metaphysical conceits are telling, effective and
original. Some of the best are to be found in Donne. In *The
Good-Morrow* he asks:

> Where can we find two better hemispheres
> Without sharp North, without declining West?

Together the lovers make one world, each being a
hemisphere. But unlike the real hemispheres, they suffer no
shortcomings; their love undergoes neither misery (sharp
North), nor cooling of affection (declining West). Donnes's
poetry features the conceit in all its varieties. Sometimes he
makes what T. S. Eliot calls 'an electric use of a condensed
conceit', as in *The Relique* where he imagines his grave being
dug up, disclosing 'a bracelet of bright hair about the bone'.
Sometimes the examples are much more elaborate, extending
over many lines and even over an entire poem. In *Good Friday,
Riding Westward,* an extended conceit is introduced by the
words 'Let man's soul be a sphere . . . '
     All Metaphysical poets make free use of the conceit. Henry
Vaughan's poem The *Retreate* is an extended one. Life is a
march or a walk; some men like to press forward ('a forward
motion love'); the speaker of the poem likes to look backward
to the source of his lost happiness, and is tempted to retrace
his steps – hence the title of the poem. There are some local
conceits: 'Before I taught my tongue to wound / My conscience with a sinful sound'; 'But ah, my soul with too much
stay / Is drunk, and staggers in the way'. One particularly
effective example conveys a strong sense of physical reality:
'But felt through all this fleshy dress / Bright shoots of ever-
lastingness'. Like his *Retreate,* Vaughan's *Showre* is built
around a Metaphysical conceit:

'Twas so, I saw thy birth: That drowsie Lake
From her faint bosom breath'd thee, the disease
Of her sick waters, and infectious Ease.
     But now at Even
     Too gross for heaven,
Thou fall'st in tears, and weep'st for thy mistake

Ah! it is so with me; oft have I prest
Heaven with a lazy breath, but fruitless this
Pierc'd not; Love only can with quick access
     Unlock the way
     When all else stray
The smoke and Exhalations of the breast.

Yet, if as thou dost melt, and with thy train
Of drops make soft the Earth, my eyes could weep
O'er my hard heart, that's bound up, and asleep,
     'Perhaps at last
     (Some such showers past)
My God would give a Sun-shine after rain.

The purpose of Vaughan's conceit is to illustrate the idea that
man's spiritual sloth and sluggishness cut him off from con-
tact with God, and that his primary need is for spiritual
regeneration. The conceit is elaborated with great skill. The
unwholesome vapours of the lake rise to become a great cloud,
which falls in 'tears' as if repenting its previous sloth; the
speaker has directed his own slothful appeals to God ('lazie
breath') but lacking the penetrating power of love, these appeals merely hovered in the air as cloudy vapours ('exhalations'). If, however, the cloud can melt in tears and soften the
earth, surely the speaker too can weep and soften his hard
heart; after some such 'showers' God may at last grant him
the light of happiness or grace.

  Long before the Metaphysical poets, the conceit was much
used in English poetry. Elizabethan love-poets commonly
employed conceits to convey the perfection of idealized mis-
tresses and to suggest the extreme nature of their own sufferings in the cause of love. A good example of the first kind is
Thomas Watson's *Passionate Centurie of Love* (1582):

> Hark you that list to hear what saint I serve
> Her yellow locks exceed the beaten gold
> Her sparkling eyes in heaven a place deserve...
> Her words are music all of silver sound...
> Each eyebrow hangs like Iris in the skies,
> Her eagle's nose is straight of stately frame...

In Sonnet 130 ('My mistress' eyes are nothing like the sun'), Shakespeare parodies these lines. An example of the use of the conceit to convey the lover's plight is Sir Thomas Wyatt's sonnet:

> Whoso list to hunt, I know where is an hind,
> But as for me, helas, I may no more.
> The vain travail hath wearied me so sore
> I am of them that farthest come behind.
> Yet may I by no means my wearied mind
> Draw from the Deer, but as she fleeth afore
> Fainting I follow, I leave off therefore,
> Since in a net I seek to hold the wind...

Shakespeare makes extensive use of the conceit throughout his plays. The word itself occurs in many of them, where it often means imagination, as for example in *Hamlet* (the Player can 'force his soul to his own conceit': II, ii, 563; the Ghost tells Hamlet that 'conceit in weakest bodies strongest works': III, iv, 115). The word can also mean wit or invention as in Falstaff's joke about Poins: 'He a good wit? Hang him baboon! His wit's as thick as Tewkesbury mustard; there's no more conceit in him than is in a mallet' (*Henry IV*, Pt. II, II, iv, 237). A well-known chain of conceits is found in Macbeth's speech on sleep 'that knits up the ravell'd sleeve of care / The death of each day's life, soe labour's bath / Balm of hurt minds . . . ' (II, ii, 36) which may be an echo of Sidney's Sonnet 39:

> Come sleep, O sleep, the certain knot of Peace,
> The baiting-place of wit, the balm of woe,
> The poor man's wealth, the prisoner's release. . . .

Examples of the conceit are to be found even in Milton. Consider the description of the sunrise in *L'Allegro*:

> Right against the Eastern gate
> Where the great Sun begins his state
> Rob'd in flames and amber light
> The clouds in thousand liveries dight
>
> (59–62)

Milton here pictures the sun, a royal personage, beginning his progress ('state') from the 'eastern gates' of his palace, attended by courtiers in the guise of clouds dressed in robes of a thousand different colours. A more 'Metaphysical' conceit is found in Milton's *Nativity Ode,* where

> the Sun in bed,
> Curtain'd with cloudy red
> Pillows his chin upon an Orient wave. . .

Eighteenth-century taste found the conceit an uncongenial figure. Johnson's remarks in his *Life of Cowley,* already quoted, are representative, as are Pope's famous lines in the *Essay on Criticism*:

> Some to Conceit alone their taste confine
> And glittering thoughts struck out at every line,
> Pleased with a work where nothing's just or fit,
> One glaring chaos and wild heap of wit   (289 ff)

In the early nineteen-twenties, T. S. Eliot turned the attention of young modern poets towards the seventeenth-century Metaphysicals. Eliot himself had already made use of Metaphysical conceits in his early poetry. The celebrated opening lines of *Prufrock,* where 'the evening is spread out against the sky / Like a patient etherised upon a table' make a good modern conceit. Lesser poets imitated the conceits of the Metaphysicals, though less memorably:

> Slugged by ungainly distance you and I
> Beneath the same stars separately lie,
> But let our worlds grow singular, and let
> Those parts be mapped some do, we would, forget. . .
>
> (Kenneth Allot, *End of A Year*)

And here is a Metaphysical conceit from a sonnet by George Barker:

> I am that land surrounding sea
> And sky: the structure of my hand
> Spreads promontories. . . .

A poem by Dylan Thomas, *After the Funeral* (*In Memory of Ann Jones*) is virtually a catalogue of conceits:

> I stand, for this memorial's sake, alone
> In the snivelling hours with dead, humped Ann
> Whose hooded, fountain heart once fell in puddles
> Round the parched worlds of Wales and drowned each Sun
> (Though this for her is a monstrous image blindly
> Magnified out of praise); her death was a still drop.
> She would not have me sinking in the holy
> Flood of her heart's fame; she would lie dumb and deep
> And need no druid of her broken body. . . .
> (Dylan Thomas, *The Poems*, ed. Daniel Jones, 1971)

See separate article on Imagery.

Bibliography: E. Holmes, *Aspects of Elizabethan Imagery*, 1929, Blackwell; G. Williamson, *The Donne Tradition*, 1930, Oxford University Press; R. M. Tuve, *Elizabethan and Metaphysical Imagery*, 1947, Cambridge University Press; Helen Gardner, *The Metaphysical Poets (Introduction to)* 1957, Penguin; H. J. C. Grierson, *'The Metaphysical Poets' in the Background to English Literature*, new ed., 1962, Barnes and Noble; M. Praz, *Studies in Seventeenth Century Imagery*, 1964, Hennessey; K. K. Ruthven, *The Conceit*, 1969, Methuen; J. B. Leishman, *The Monarch of Wit*, 1967, Hutchinson; *The Art of Marvell's Poetry*, 1968, Hutchinson.

Convention

Little in the way of extended comment on any literary genre, work or character can make much sense without reference to convention. In ordinary usage, a convention is variously defined as 'an agreement or covenant between parties' and 'general agreement or consent, as embodied in any accepted usage, standard, etc.' In the case of literary convention, the agreement is between writers and readers. At a very basic level, writer and reader are in tacit agreement that the words and idioms used in a given work have certain commonly-accepted meanings; without the possibility of such understanding, communication between them would clearly not be possible. The writer's use of words and idioms is to this extent conventional. Again, if a poet calls one of his works a ballad or an elegy, his reader assumes with justification that the poem will conform to some extent at least to certain commonly-accepted norms which traditionally govern these forms. Readers will expect sonnets to have fourteen lines and a certain rhyming-scheme, ballads to have a particular style and metre, dramatic monologues to feature a single speaker, a situation and an implied listener. Odes are conventionally complex and elaborate in their stanza structure, epic style is conventionally remote from common speech. The list might be extended to include all literary forms. The very division of poems into odes, epics, ballads, elegies and so on is in itself conventional, and implies an acceptance of the idea that each literary form has its characteristic conventions.

Some conventions, expecially dramatic ones, are so universal and taken so much for granted that we can forget that they are conventions. A room with four walls is conventionally represented on a stage as a set with three walls. Serious characters in Elizabethan and Jacobean drama speak in blank verse; those in Restoration tragedy and in French heroic drama speak in rhyming couplets. These are freely accepted conventions. Again, the soliloquy and the aside are basic conventions of Shakespearian drama. Such studies as M. C. Bradbrook's *Themes and Conventions of Elizabethan Tragedy* illustrate both the great number of conventions governing all aspects of the plays, and the importance of recognizing these conventions if we are not to misinterpret many aspects of character, incident and presentation.

In Elizabethan comedy, one of the most obvious conventional devices, used again and again, was the assumption of male disguise by female characters (*As You Like It* and *Twelfth Night,* for example). The impenetrability of such disguise was another convention. A great deal of space has been devoted to ingenious attempts to account for the motives of some Shakespearian characters, much of it to little effect. A recognition of the conventional way in which Shakespeare motivates his characters (however realistically he presents them) would save a lot of needless discussion. A Shakespearian character (Leontes, Iago, for example) who is behaving conventionally (according to type) will need no motivation at all. Iago, as M. C. Bradbrook points out, 'is plainly a villain, as he is at pains to expound in soliloquy. Villains are villains. There is no need to ask why. They are as they are. Besides this, he is an Italian, and therefore it goes without saying that he is treacherous, jealous and Machiavellian' (*Themes and Conventions,* 1960 edn., p. 65). Drama and prose fiction have, since the earliest times, featured a limited range of conventional character types, usually described as stock characters. In comedy, one of the most enduring of such conventional types is the *miles gloriosus* or military braggart, a famous example being Shakespeare's Falstaff. Comic plot is often manipulated in conventional ways: unlikely conversions, miraculous transformations, providential interventions are frequently met with in comedy.

An understanding of a conventional Elizabethan plot form throws significant light on *Hamlet,* and makes a good deal of traditional comment on character and play appear beside the point. As Helen Gardner points out, 'The essence of any tragedy of revenge is that its hero has not created the situation in which he finds himself and out of which the tragedy arises. . . . The exposition of such plays does not display the hero taking a fatal step, but the hero confronted with appalling facts. . . But in the Elizabethan revenge plays it is not merely the initial situation which is created by the villain. The development also comes about through his initiative. It is not the result of a successfully carried out scheme of the revenger. The revenger takes an opportunity unconsciously provided for him by the villain.' (*The Business of Criticism,* 1959, p. 41).

An appeal to dramatic convention can throw useful light on some of the more notorious character problems met with in Shakespearian drama, and confronted at such tedious length in discussions of it. One feature of Shakespeare's presentation of character that has been much misunderstood is the tendency of some of the major figures to emphasise their own virtues or their own vices. The most obvious examples are Julius Caesar, Brutus and Iago. Brutus, for example, frequently draws attention to his own disinterestedness and honour, his high moral standing; Caesar talks in exaggerated terms of his own fearlessness and constancy. Iago openly declares his villainy. One's natural reaction is to find Brutus and Caesar embarrassingly boastful and Iago deeply cynical. A different view emerges, however, if one sees such utterances as examples of Shakespeare's use of conventional Elizabethan methods of character presentation. Shakespeare and his contemporaries commonly let us know what a character is really like by letting the character himself tell us directly. The villain, in other words, is to be a villain, and the noble character is to appear noble, from whichever side one looks at them. We are simply to take them at their word. The convention of self-explanation may appear primitive, but one of its obvious aims is to avoid misrepresentation of the main features of the characters and of the action, to avoid confusion of ethical values. When the ghost of Hamlet's father talks of Claudius as a man 'whose natural gifts were poor to those of mine' (I, v, 51) we need not convict him of boastfulness or self-complacency; he is merely giving factual information in a conventional way.

Even the oldest conventions still survive in modern drama. In *Murder in the Cathedral* T. S. Eliot makes use of a wide range of traditional dramatic conventions. His use of the Chorus and of the messenger is derived from the universal practice of ancient Greek drama. He uses a number of liturgical conventions with striking appropriateness. He enlarges the function of the Greek chorus in the light of the Christian liturgy so that it becomes a choir, articulating the voices of Christian worshippers. The play depends for much of its effect on the conventional relationship of priests, choir and congregation.

In Becket's Christmas sermon we find a fusion of liturgical and dramatic conventions; this familiar form of direct address provided Eliot with a ready-made and acceptable convention for soliloquy: a useful device in a drama of spiritual revelation.

The major poetic conventions are discussed in the articles on the sonnet, the pastoral elegy, the ballad, the dramatic monologue, and the epic. It should be emphasised that the word 'conventional' applied to a literary work should not be regarded as a term of abuse. No convention is good or bad in itself; everything depends on how it is used. In successful poems, there is a fruitful tension between the demands of the conventional form on the one hand, and the poet's quest for individual expression, freedom and originality on the other. The sonnet provides several good examples of this. Its restrictive conventions (fixed length, demanding rhyme-scheme, conventional metrical form) present a powerful and stimulating challenge to the complex development of themes, as well as to the achievement of individuality, richness of imagery, variety of mood and tone. Again, the pastoral elegy, one of the most conventional of all poetic forms, can be a dull, routine affair. *Lycidas,* the supreme English achievement in the genre, succeeds because Milton is able to animate the conventions he uses, to make them the convincing expression of universal human feelings, attitudes and problems.

Conventions, as Christopher Ricks remarks, 'usually grow up because of some basic truth or common attitude which they crystallize, but then it is also true that this makes them all too useful to anyone who wants to fake a basic truth or a common attitude. . . . A literary convention well used is like that useful convention short-hand. Ill-used, it is forgery'. (*English Poetry and Prose,* 1540–1674, 1970, p. 258). Many readers of *Lycidas* may wonder why Milton stages his mourner as an 'uncouth swain', and the subject of his poem as a shepherd, and why he preserves his elaborate pastoral machinery to the end. The short answer is that he is writing in a tradition as old as the Greek poet Theocritus, and that his deference to traditional forms (a characteristic of Renaissance writers) made it unthinkable for him to write an elegy in any but conventional terms. Renaissance poets tended to be more interested in the profitable imitation of their classical predecessors than worried about how such imitation might cramp their individuality and limit their freedom. But the fact that so many poets wrote elegies after the manner of Theocritus cannot be accounted for simply in terms of the unquestioning acceptance of a classical tradition. The form evolved by Theocritus must correspond (or have seemed to many poets to correspond) to what Ricks calls 'some basic truth or common attitude', must have appeared the inevitable form for this kind of subject. In answer to the question why Theocritus presented himself and his friends in a pastoral guise, one of his editors suggests that 'first, the Greek mind associated poetry directly with music; and secondly, Greek herdsmen were then, as they are still, players and singers. The poets of his day, some of whom dealt with country life, would naturally appear, to a country-loving poet like Theocritus, the literary counterparts, so to speak, of the herdsmen, and their poetry in some sense the art-form of the herdsman's folk-music' (J. M. Edwards, *The Greek Bucolic Poets*, Harvard U.P. 1937, p. xv).

By the middle of the eighteenth century, English poets and critics had come to regard the traditional pastoral conventions as no longer adequate to express their feelings or ideas, as impossibly remote and artificial. This is the basis of Johnson's hostile comments on *Lycidas* in his Life of Milton. As Johnson sees it, whatever images the pastoral can supply 'are long ago exhausted; and its inherent improbability always forces dissatisfaction on the mind'.

See separate articles on Ballad, Comedy, Epic, Pastoral Elegy, Sonnet, Tragedy etc.

Bibliography: J. L. Lowes, *Convention and Revolt in Poetry*, 1919, Constable; E. E. Stoll, *Poets and Playrights*, 1930, Oxford University Press; M. C. Bradbrook, *Themes and Conventions of Elizabethan Tragedy*, 1935, Cambridge University Press; C. S. Lewis, *A Preface to Paradise Lost*, 1942, Oxford University Press; H. Levin, *Perspectives of Criticism*, 1950, Oxford University Press; N. Frye, *Anatomy of Criticism*, 1957, Oxford University Press; Helen Gardner, *The Business of Criticism*, 1959, Oxford University Press; G. Hough, *Reflections on a Literary Revolution*, 1960, Catholic University of America Press; W. W. Lawrence, *Shakespeare's Problem Comedies*, 1960, Ungar; R. Williams, *Drama from Ibsen to Eliot*, 1964, Penguin; Samuel Johnson, *Johnson on Shakespeare*, 1968, Yale University Press.

Dramatic

The term 'dramatic' is used of various literary works besides plays: we speak, for example, of dramatic monologues and dramatic lyrics. In its original meaning, the word 'drama' implied a thing done; drama is commonly described as 'character in action'. The author of a dramatic poem creates or evokes a situation, which takes its meaning and interest from a specific context. Expectations are aroused, often by means of a particularly arresting or exciting opening, as is the case, for example, with so many Metaphysical poems:

> Before I sigh my last gasp, let me breath,
> Great love, some legacies. . . .
>
> (Donne, *The Will*)

> I struck the board, and cried, No more.
> I will abroad. . . .
>
> (Herbert, *The Collar*)

> I saw Eternity the other night . . .
> (Vaughan, *The World*)

The subject is something for the reader to feel concerned about and closely involved in: drama implies tension, suspense, conflict, excitement. The dramatic poet causes us to enter into an experience or situation by bringing it vividly to life:

> Busie old foole, unruly Sunne,
> Why dost thou thus,
> Through windowes, and through curtains call on us?
> Must to thy motions lovers seasons run?
> Sawcy pedantic wretch, goe chide
> Late schoole-boyes, and sour prentices,
> Goe tell Court-huntsmen, that the King will ride,
> Call countrey ants to harvest offices;
> Love, all alike, no season knowes, nor clyme,
> Nor houres, dayes, months, which are the rags of time.
>
> (Donne, *The Sunne Rising*)

In The *Goodmorrow*, Donne vividly conveys a sense of joyful excitement in his enactment of the awakening of the lovers to a new life; in *The Collar*, Herbert creates a sense of immediate action, of agitated struggle. The sense of immediacy is central to dramatic literature: we must be made to feel that what we read is happening now. The medium of dramatic poetry is dramatic language, the movement and intonation of which are those of the talking voice. The dramatic speech of any age must never be out of harmony with the current style of familiar speech. Shakespeare's Blank Verse was in close accord with the everyday language of Shakespeare's time, which gave it a living, vibrant quality; now that the everyday language has changed, Shakespeare's dramatic verse has inevitably lost some of its power. Milton's epic blank verse, on the other hand, can never have been regarded as preserving the idioms and rhythms of living speech, except at isolated moments.

Dramatic poetry presupposes objectivity on the part of the poet, who presents a situation, action or experience as something existing in its own right, and not as a reflection of his own feelings. It is important to remember that the speakers in dramatic poems are not to be identified with the poets themselves, any more than are the various characters in a poetic drama. It can be seriously misleading to read such poems with a view to compiling biographical details. To use a famous distinction proposed by T. S. Eliot, the man who suffers is not the same as the mind which creates. The speakers in dramatic poems act out roles. Donne's love-poems, for example, are like performances by an actor who wears a variety of masks for a variety of occasions and situations, none of which necessarily arises from the poet's life or corresponds to any of its particular circumstances, or is intended to reflect his attitudes. It would be absurd to claim that the Duke in Browning's *My Last Duchess* stands for his creator, or that Prufrock is Eliot.

It may be of value to point to some examples of poems which are clearly non-dramatic. We do not, for example, expect to find dramatic qualities in reflective, meditative, mystical poems; in poems which are purely descriptive, or in poems written in relaxed, incantatory language whose effect is to convey the reader far away from reality. The opening lines

of Milton's *Paradise Lost* exhibit a use of language which is
clearly not dramatic:

> Of Man's first disobedience, and the fruit
> Of that forbidden tree whose mortal taste
> Brought death into the World, and all our woe,
> With loss of Eden, till one greater Man
> Restore us, and regain the blissful seat,
> Sing, Heavenly Muse. . . .

The rhythms of this passage are those of a formal oration and
of a solemn prayer; the urgency and immediacy of dramatic
speech are notably absent. The clause-structure differs
radically from that of the spoken language, while the main
verb does not appear until the sixth line. Milton is enacting a
solemn, deliberate, stately ritual, for the purposes of which
dramatic speech would be quite irrelevant. Many of the great
Romantic odes (those of Coleridge, Wordsworth, Keats and
Shelley) are admirable examples of non-dramatic poetry.
Shelley appropriately describes the verse of his *Ode to the West
Wind* as incantatory.

To illustrate the dramatic use of language by a poet not
writing for the theatre, one might choose almost any of
Donne's dramatic lyrics. Here is a famous passage from his
Third Satire:

>   On a huge hill
> Cragged, and steep, Truth stands, and hee that will
> Reach her, about must, and about must goe;
> And what the hills suddenness resists, winne so;
> Yet strive so, that before age, deaths twilight,
> Thy soule rest, for none can worke in that night. . . .

On the dramatic quality of this passage F. R. Leavis comments: 'The words seem to do what they say; a very obvious
example of what, in more or less subtle forms, is pervasive being given in the image of reaching that the reader has to enact
when he passes from the second to the third line' (*Revaluation*,
p. 55). A reading of the sonnet 'Batter My Heart' imposes
movements on the reader similar to those described above by
Leavis. A further example of 'enactment' is Hamlet's 'And in

this harsh world draw thy breath in pain' (V, ii, 348). As the eighteenth-century critic Daniel Webb pointed out, 'the breath actually labours to get through this line'. Here are the opening lines of Pope's *Epistle to Arbuthnot:*

> Shut, shut the door, good John! fatigued, I said,
> Tie up the knocker, say I'm sick, I'm dead.
> The Dog-star rages! nay 'tis past a doubt,
> All Bedlam, or Parnassus, is let out:
> Fire in each eye, and papers in each hand,
> They rave, recite, and madden round the land.
> What walls can guard me, or what shades can hide?
> They pierce my thickets, through my Grot they glide;
> By land, by water, they renew the charge;
> They stop the chariot, and they board the barge.
> No place is sacred, not the Church is free;
> Even Sunday shines no Sabbath-day to me
> Then from the Mint walks forth the man of rhyme,
> Happy to catch me just at dinner-time.

These colloquially dramatic lines vividly create a situation, and at the same time reveal something of the temperament and character of the speaker. His cherished privacy is being infringed on by a band of poets both crazy and bad ('All Bedlam, or Parnassus is let out'). He is safe from their unwelcome attentions neither at home nor in church. Their sore task does not divide the Sunday from the week. He ruefully recognizes that all avenues of escape are closed. The impatient exclamations arise directly from the situation (the unwarranted assault on the speaker's privacy) which is *presented*, not merely described, in terms of a siege. The active verbs have an important function here. The agitated, impatient movement of the verse enacts the troubled movements of the speaker's mind, and implies as an accompaniment a set of restless, exasperated gestures and facial expressions.

Shakespeare depends on dramatic poetry to achieve many of the effects a modern playwright might strive to achieve by means of music and scenery and a battery of sound-effects. Consider, for example, the storm-scenes in *King Lear*. The actors in this scene not only carry forward the story but also *create* the storm; they do not simply describe it. The chief actor

must impersonate both Lear and the storm. Lear's great
speech, 'Blow, winds and crack your cheeks! rage! blow! (III,
ii) is, as Granville Barker pointed out, 'no mere description of
a storm, but in music and imaginative suggestion a dramatic
creating of the storm itself'. (Preface to *King Lear,* 1963 edn.,
p. 7).

The best dramatic speech involves a correspondence
between the actor's words and his gestures. Macbeth's great
last-act soliloquies show how Shakespeare facilitates such a
correspondence:

> To-morrow and to-morrow and to-morrow,
> Creeps in this petty pace from day to day
> To the last syllable of recorded time;
> And all our yesterdays have lighted fools
> The way to dusty death. Out, out, brief candle!
> Life's but a walking shadow, a poor player
> That struts and frets his hour upon the stage
> And then is heard no more. It is a tale
> Told by an idiot, full of sound and fury,
> Signifying nothing.
>
> (V, v, 19 ff)

The actor's movements and gestures give visual impact to the
words. The actor is pacing the stage as he speaks of 'this petty
pace' and of the player strutting and fretting his hour upon
the stage, which he gestures to as the place of 'dusty death'.
But it is not enough for the dialogue to correspond closely to
the actor's movements and gestures: the language itself must
convey a sense of dynamic action. This is present in the soliloquy just quoted and in Pope's *Epistle to Arbuthnot,* but it is
largely absent from Becket's climactic speech in *Murder in the
Cathedral.*

> Now is my way clear, now is the meaning plain:
> Temptation shall not come in this kind again.
> The last temptation is the greatest treason:
> To do the right deed for the wrong reason . . .

It is obvious that comparatively few elements of this speech
convey any sense of action or urgency; there is little or no

implication of movement. The speech is largely static in quality, and it is not until the last few lines that a sense of urgency becomes apparent: 'Now my good Angel, whom God appoints / To be my guardian / Hover over the swords' points'.

Bibliography: F. R. Leavis, *Revaluation,* 1936, Chatto; A. R. Thompson, *The Anatomy of Drama,* 1942, Cambridge University Press; L. C. Knights, *Explorations,* 1946, Chatto; H. Granville Barker, *Prefaces to Shakespeare,* 2 vols. 1958, Batsford; *On Dramatic Method,* 1960, Peter Smith (Gloucester. Mass); A. Nicoll, *The Theatre and Dramatic Theory,* 1962, Harrap; U. Ellis-Fermer, *The Frontiers of Drama,* 1964, Methuen; E. Bentley, *The Life of the Drama,* 1965, Methuen; G. Wilson Knight, *Shakespearian Production,* 1968, Routledge; F. Fergusson, *The Idea of A Theatre,* 1949, Oxford University Press; 1949 hardback, paperback 1968 Princeton University Press both editions; C. Leech, *The Dramatist's Experience,* 1970, Chatto; S. Wells, *Literature and Drama,* 1970, Routledge; S. W. Dawson, *Drama and the Dramatic,* 1970, Methuen.

Dramatic Monologue

The dramatic monolgue was perfected by Tennyson (*St Simeon Stylytes, Ulysses*) and Browning (*My Last Duchess, Caliban Upon Setebos, Fra Lippo Lippi, An Epistle, Andrea del Sarto*), and used with distinction by some major twentieth-century poets such as Yeats (*Crazy Jane* poems, for example) and Eliot (*Prufrock, Portrait of a Lady, Journey of the Magi, A Song for Simeon, Marina*). The essential features of the dramatic monologue are easily set forth. There is a speaker, who is not the poet, and whose speech the poem is, and also a listener or listeners, whose presence in the poem we infer from what the speaker says. The speaker's utterance is a response to an occasion or event, of crucial importance in his career. There is some interplay between speaker and listener.

The main object of the dramatic monologue is to provide an understanding of the speaker, of his character and temperament, and this implies a degree of sympathy for him, whatever his moral nature. In some of Browning's dramatic monologues, for example, where the speakers are villains, reprobates, and otherwise morally reprehensible, there is a powerful tension between the sympathy generated for them by the poem and the reader's moral judgement. *My Last Duchess* is a good example. Here the speaker is an amoral Renaissance Duke who has unjustly put his last Duchess to death and is arranging another marriage for himself through an ambasador, mainly for the sake of the dowry. But a necessary condition of reading the poem is the willingness of the reader to understand the Duke, even to sympathise with him. This is possible firstly because we are given the facts of the case from his point of view, and secondly because we admire him, however grudgingly, for his power of intellect and will, for his sheer effrontery, his aristocratic contempt for his listener's intelligence, and his highly developed artistic sense. Browning was fond of making a case for points of view which from an orthodox standpoint could only be regarded as immoral, and since the dramatic monologue requires sympathy for the speaker as a basic condition of reading the poem, it is an excellent vehicle for dramatising a morally difficult, even indefensible, case. The reader takes up the speaker's view of things in order to understand him, and he suspends moral judgement.

It is easy to confuse the dramatic monologue with the soliloquy. An obvious difference is that whereas the soliloquist addresses himself, the speaker of the dramatic monologue has a listener within the poem, whose presence is always to be inferred from the nature of the speaker's address. In Eliot's *Prufrock,* however, the speaker does not address himself to an independent listener: he addresses his other self (the 'you' of line one). It is also necessary to distinguish between the dramatic monologue and the dramatic lyric. In the latter, we may or may not be forced to the conclusion that the speaker and the poet are the same person (see the separate article on the lyric). The speaker of the dramatic monologue, on the other hand, is not to be identified with the poet. Again, in some dramatic lyrics, (many of Donne's, for example), the interest lies less in the speaker's revelation of his character (an essential feature of the dramatic monologue) than in the ingenuity of his argument.

The dramatic monologue is really one voice of a dialogue, a voice which conveys as much as possible of the speaker's life and experience. Another way to regard it is in relation to the drama proper. In a play, we subordinate the various points of view represented by the various speakers to the general perspective. A dramatic monologue is like a brief play in which the central character is allowed to become so dominant that we see everything through his eyes, and the play as a mere episode in his career. To this extent, a dramatic monologue is an incomplete play, the whole weight of which falls on the speaker.

A significant feature of the dramatic monologue is that the motives for which the characters speak cannot be adequately accounted for by the dramatic situation. The monologue arises only partly as a response to the situation; it can be seen as the occasion for an illuminating review of the speaker's life, the expression of his ambitions, his obsessions, his triumphs, his fears. A dramatic monologue differs from a speech in a drama in that the speaker in the former seldom, if ever, accomplishes anything by his utterance, and is resigned to this from the start, whereas in the latter, one expects the utterance to alter events to some extent. But the question then arises, if the speaker of the dramatic monologue knows that he will not really achieve anything by his speech, why does he speak at all? The answer, in many cases, is that he speaks in order to learn something about himself. Its exploratory form helps to account for the tone of improvisation in most dramatic monologues, the speaker's intense concentration on what he is saying, and his relative indifference to the listener's response. The song of the title of Eliot's poem *The Love Song of J Alfred Prufrock* is sung for nobody's benefit but the singer's own. In this poem, the situation, such as it is, can hardly be said to account for what the speaker has to say. In fact, he does not really advert directly to the situation at all, and what he has to say is not even contemporaneous with the situation (the posing of the question) which never becomes actual and is presented either as anticipation ('there will be time'; 'how should I begin') or as recollection ('would it have been worth it after all'). Eliot's poem is an unusual dramatic monologue in some respects. In other poems written in the form, the listener is a second presence. In Eliot's Prufrock's other self (the 'you' of line one) is the auditor who observes Prufrock's activities. But while the choice of the speaker's other self as auditor may appear odd, it really involves a recognition on Eliot's part of an essential feature of the dramatic monologue: that the speaker's utterances go beyond the dramatic situation and beyond the listener to some projection of the speaker himself, because he is speaking in order to understand himself, or something about himself. In his study of the form, Robert Langbaum points out that it is the speaker's ultimate purpose that accounts for the curious style of address of the dramatic monologue: 'Not only does the speaker direct his address outward as in dialogue but the style of address gives the effect of a closed circuit, with the speaker directing his address outward in order that it may return with a meaning he was not aware of when sending it forth. I say a closed circuit because the utterance seems to be directed only obliquely at the ostensible auditor, and seems never to reach its ultimate goal with him. Nor does the essential interchange take place with the auditor; for even where the auditor's remarks are implied, the speaker never learns anything from them and they do not change the meaning of the utterance. If the speaker represents one voice of a dialogue, then his other self is the essential second voice in that it sends back his own voice with a difference'. (*The Poetry of Experience* 1957, p. 191).

While Browning's *My Last Duchess* is a perfect specimen of the dramatic monologue, Eliot's *Prufrock* barely qualifies for the description. There is in the latter only the implication of the present tense situation, and if this were taken away the poem would cease to be a dramtic monologue and become a lyric. There is only just enough of dramatic situation (the vague business of the visit and the putting of the question) to serve as the excuse or the occasion for Prufrock's self-projection and self-discovery. We realize how exiguous the situational material really is when we remember that we know nothing of Prufrock's lady, their relationship or what may be supposed to pass between them. Eliot's poem illustrates in extreme form what is found in all dramatic monologues: the subordination of the situation itself to what the speaker can extract from it, its use as the means by which he learns what he reveals about himself.

Eliot's successful experiments in the form lend weight to his observations on its nature and problems in a lecture called *The Three Voices of Poetry*. The first of the three voices 'is the voice of the poet talking to himself – or to nobody. The second is the voice of the poet addressing an audience, whether large or small. The third is the voice of the poet when he attempts to create a dramatic character speaking in verse; when he is saying, not what he would say in his own person, but only what he can say within the limits of one imaginary character addressing another imaginary character' (*On Poetry and Poets*, 1957, p. 89). This third voice is that of the poet who writes dramatic monologues. The major problem facing such a poet is, as Eliot puts it, 'to extract the poetry from the character, rather than impose his poetry upon it' (Ibid., p. 95). The trouble is that the author is just as likely to identify the character with himself as himself with the character (since he doesn't, in the nature of the case, have to identify himself with some other character replying to the first). Eliot concludes that Browning in his monologues is talking aloud through his characters: 'When we listen to a play by Shakespeare, we listen not to Shakespeare but to his characters; when we read a dramatic monologue by Browning, we cannot suppose that we are listening to any other voice that that of Browning himself' (Ibid., p. 96).

This last remark stands in need of qualification. There are some monologues in which Browning's dramatic sense is strong enough to enable him to create characters who are not mere mouthpieces for his own opinions and attitudes. *My Last Duchess* is a good example. When we listen to the Duke in this poem we are not in the least conscious of the voice of Browning. The same is true of the speaker in *The Bishop Orders his Tomb*. Browning's command of dramatic objectivity in some of the other monologues is less assured. One obvious example is *Fra Lippo Lippi*. Here Browning creates a lively, sympathetic character, but far too often through the monologue uses him as a mouthpiece for his own views on art, simply talking through him, not extracting his appropriate utterance from him. This criticism might also be applied to *Caliban Upon Setebos* and *Bishop Blougram's Apology*.

See separate article on Dramatic.

Bibliography: M. W. MacCallum *'The Dramatic Monologue in the Victorian Period' Proceedings of the British Academy, 1924–25*, Oxford University Press; B. Fuson, *Browning and His English Predecessors in the Dramatic Monologue*, 1948, University of Iowa; T. S. Eliot, *'The Three Voices of Poetry' in On Poetry and Poets*, 1957, Faber; R. Langbaum, *The Poetry of Experience*, 1957, Chatto; P. Honan, *Browning's Characters*, 1961, Yale University Press; P. Drew, ed., *Robert Browning: A Collection of Critical Essays*, 1966, Methuen; Ian Jack, *Browning's Major Poetry*, 1973, Oxford University Press.

Epic and Mock-Heroic

In the section dealing with the Ballad, it was pointed out the sophisticated literary ballads written by learned poets were composed in conscious imitation of the traditional folk ballads or popular street ballads of pre-literate or semi-literate societies. Two kinds of epic may be distinguished on the basis of a similar kind of distinction. The earliest kind of epic, variously described as traditional, folk or primary epic, was fashioned by a literary artist from historical, mythological and legendary material which he derived from the oral traditions of his race. The greatest primary epics of classical times are Homer's *Illiad* and *Odyssey*. The major Anglo-Saxon example is *Beowulf*. These traditional primary epics were later imitated by the learned, sophisticated writers of 'literary' or secondary epics. The great classical example of the secondary epic is the Roman Virgil's *Aeneid*. This was the prime literary influence on the single great English secondary epic, Milton's *Paradise Lost*. Since *Paradise Lost* is, in fact, the only major English example of the literary epic in poetry, it is, perhaps, best to concentrate attention on the ways in which Milton's poem embodies the traditional epic conventions.

The epic poem is the most ambitious and demanding of all literary enterprises. Milton is conscious that in *Paradise Lost* he is undertaking 'things unattempted yet in prose or rhyme' (Book I, 16), but in encompassing this he finds it necessary to trace the celestial cycle from the fall of the rebel angels through the fall of man and the redemption to a panoramic survey of human history to a vision of the Last Judgment. All this material is deployed to illustrate the working out of a vast Providential design in human history.

Paradise Lost is a highly conventional literary epic. An account of its conventional features is largely an account of the conventions of the epic form. The traditional epic hero is a figure of immense importance to his nation, often having divine associations (Virgil's Aeneas, for example, is the son of the goddess Aphrodite). In the case of *Paradise Lost,* the identity of the hero is a problem which has led to much knocking about of brains among critics. Christ is sometimes described as the hero because, being both God and man, he is the figure who most perfectly unites the human and divine strands of the poem. Against this, there is the fact that Christ's appearances are comparatively few, and that Milton's presentation is such that he does not exert anything like the dominance one expects from an epic hero. The same reason might be urged against regarding Adam as the hero, even though he stands for the entire human race. Satan, the official villain of the epic, is invested with a greater range of classic heroic qualities than any other figure in the poem: outstanding physical powers, courage, fortitude in adversity, resourcefulness, an unrivalled talent for inspired leadership, and so on. But the case against the common assumption that Milton thought of Satan as the hero of the epic is based on (a) the fact that so to regard him would be to accuse Milton of subverting the thesis of *Paradise Lost*, which was 'to justify the ways of God to men', and (b) the fact that Satan puts his heroic qualities to most unheroic use, and as the poem proceeds, becomes more and more degenerate. But the identity of the hero is less important than the fact that epic heroism is exemplified – in various characters – to a high degree in *Paradise Lost,* and that the heroic tone is the dominant one. Christ's unselfish offer of himself as a sacrifice for mankind and Satan's thrilling journey through Chaos in search of the newly-created world are episodes in the true heroic tradition. Another feature of classical epic preserved by Milton is the heroic character of the war in Heaven, the descriptions of which have ample precedents in the epics of Homer and Virgil.

Local epic conventions include an initial announcement by the poet of the argument or subject of his poem, followed by the invocation of the muse (in Milton's Christian epic the muse is the Holy Spirit). Further, the poet begins his narrative not at the chronological start of the action but in the middle, at a crucial stage. Thus *Paradise Lost* opens with a picture of Satan and his followers in Hell. Then there are the conventional catalogues of the names of some of the major epic figures (Book I of *Paradise Lost,* lines 392 ff.), followed by a debate in which these characters are allowed to reveal their contrasting attitudes to the business in hand (*Paradise Lost,* Book II, 43 ff.).

A major feature of epic is its special style, which is dictated by the nature of the form. Epic, whether primary or secondary, is highly stylised, formal and ceremonial. If an epic were to have a public recitation, the occasion would be a solemn ritual one. The style appropriate to this kind of poem is clearly one which is remote from everyday speech either in diction or rhythm: a formal, liturgical style with its own characteristically stylised movement and appropriate 'poetic' diction. The style of Milton's *Paradise Lost* (the 'Grand Style') is distinguished by these qualities. It is a learned style, rich in allusions of varying subtlety to all kinds of great literature, sacred and profane, influenced by classical Latin in its syntax and diction. There has, since the nineteen-thirties, been a strong tendency among critics to contrast (unfavourably to Milton) the ritual style of *Paradise Lost* with the conversational style of Donne and the dramatic style of Shakespeare. But such contrasts ignore the demands of the epic form. An epic style is narrative, rhetorical, continuously elevated; it cannot go very far in the direction of being colloquial or witty without ceasing to be epic, or shift too far from its major heroic key without throwing the poem off balance.

Something must be said about Milton's significant departure in *Paradise Lost* from traditional epic values. In Book I, Satan is the classic epic hero, who displays the qualities always associated with this figure: bravery, resourcefulness, leadership, indomitable pride. He and his followers are associated with all the fabled military heroes of ancient epic and romance, those who fought at Thebes and Illium, British and Armoric knights, the Crusaders and their enemies. It is they, in other words, who are allowed the virtual monopoly of warlike heroism. But in *Paradise Lost,* military success is not presented by Milton as the highest kind of achievement, although he is conscious that epic poets had always made it seem as if it were. His rejection of this tradition, and his own version of the true epic theme, are set forth at the beginning of Book IX:

> Since first this subject for heroic song
> Pleased me long choosing, and beginning late;
> Not sedulous by nature to indite
> Wars, hitherto the only argument

Heroic deemed, chief mastery to dissect
With long and tedious havoc fabled knights
In battles feigned; the better fortitude
Of patience and heroic martyrdom
Unsung; or to describe races and games,
Or tilting furniture, emblazoned shields...

(lines 25–34)

The relationship between Satan's status in *Paradise Lost* and
Milton's rejection of traditional 'heroic' values is aptly
described by Stanley Fish: 'One of the more misleading questions that has been asked of *Paradise Lost* is, is Satan really
courageous? Misleading, because it assumes that an answer,
one way or the other, will help to settle a great issue, the identity of the poem's hero; whereas, in truth, the concept of
heroism implied in the question is not the norm that Milton
would have us accept. In an important way epic heroism, of
which Satan is a noteworthy instance, is the antithesis of
Christian heroism, and a large part of the poem is devoted to
distinguishing between the two and showing the superiority of
the latter. Since this involves the debunking of an ideal the
reader brings with him from other epics, the reading experience is educative and disillusioning'. ('Standing Only:
Christian Heroism and Paradise Lost', *Critical Quarterly*, IX,
No. 2, p. 162).

The debate about Milton's epic style has been referred to
above. The most celebrated defence of this style in terms of
genre is that of C. S. Lewis: 'The style of Virgil and Milton
arises as the solution of a very definite problem. The Secondary epic aims at an even higher solemnity than the Primary;
but it has lost all those external aids to solemnity which the
Primary enjoyed. There is no robed and garlanded aoidos, no
altar, not even a feast in a hall – only a private person reading
a book in an armchair. Yet somehow or other, that private
person must be made to feel that he is assisting at an august
ritual, for if he does not, he will not be receptive of the true
epic exhilaration. The sheer writing of the poem, therefore,
must now do, of itself, what the whole occasion helped to for
Homer. The Virgilian and Miltonic style is there to compen-
sate for – to counteract – the privacy and informality of silent
reading in a man's own study. Every judgment on it which

does not realize this will be inept. To blame it for being
ritualistic or incantatory, for lacking intimacy or the speaking
voice, is to blame it for being just what it intends to be and
ought to be. It is like damning an opera or an oratorio because
the personages sing instead of speaking' (*A Preface to Paradise
Lost*, 1942, p. 39).

So profoundly serious a form as epic, particularly an example like *Paradise Lost,* inevitably lends itself to parody and
burlesque. The comic possibilities inherent in the application
of the solemn style of Milton's poem to trivial subjects are obvious, and many later poets exploited these with varying
degrees of success. The classic example of mock-heroic or
mock-epic poetry is Pope's *Rape of the Lock,* the brilliant, witty
outcome of Pope's study of the great epics, English and classical. It is important to observe that in Pope's poem the
language and ideas of solemn and dignified works like *Paradise
Lost* are put to comic use, not in order to ridicule these works
(see below), but to underline the absurdity of making a
serious issue of such a trivial incident as the one which inspired *The Rape of the Lock.*

The poem was founded on an incident from life, involving
two families with whom Pope was on friendly terms, the
Petres and the Fermors. Lord Robert Petre, the Baron of the
poem, had taken a lock of hair from the head of Arabella Fer-
mor, Pope's Belinda. The result was a breach between the
families, and the suggestion to Pope that he should, by writing a poem, help to make a jest of the episode, and 'laugh
them together again'. By writing of the theft of Belinda's hair
in the same tones as Milton assumed to relate the fall of mankind, Pope is able to reduce the affair to its proper proportions. 'The use of pompous expression for low actions', Pope
declared, 'is the perfection of the mock-epic'. He borrowed
more than the heroic style from the traditional epic. The gran-
diose description (Canto I, 121–48); the long simile (Canto V,
45–52); the formal speech (Canto IV, 113–20), and the battle
between the sexes, waged with hatpins, snuff and metaphors
(V, 37–86), are inspired mimicry of epic conventions, whose
elevated origins may be studied in *Paradise Lost.* Even Ariel
and the Sylphs (Canto III, 135–52), guardians of female virtue, recall the good angels of Milton's epic. The traditional
epic voyage (Satan's in *Paradise Lost*) is appropriately reduced

by Pope to the dimensions of a boat journey on the Thames (Canto II).

In considering the relationship between epic poetry and mock-heroic, it is important to bear in mind that if Augustan poets like Pope and Dryden saw their mock-heroic poems as parodies of epic, their understanding of the term 'parody' was not the modern one. By parody, Augustan writers understood 'a kind of writing in which the words of an author or his thoughts are taken, and by a slight change adapted to some new purpose' (Johnson's Dictionary). They did not set out, as a modern parodist might, to ridicule the style and conventions of a well-established poetic kind by means of exaggeration or distortion. Ian Jack points out that 'while modern critics often think of a mock-heroic poem as a satire on epic, the Augustans laid the emphasis elsewhere . . . The writers who did ridicule the epic were the authors of burlesques and travesties . . . In mock-heroic a dignified genre is turned to witty use without being cheapened in any way. The poet has an opportunity of ridiculing through incongruity, and of affording his reader the sophisticated pleasure of recognizing ironical parallels to familiar passages in Homer and Virgil' (*Augustan Satire*, 1945 edn., p. 78).

Bibliography: C. S. Lewis, *A Preface to Paradise Lost*, 1942, Oxford University Press; H. T. Swedenberg, *The Theory of the Epic in England 1650–1800*. 1944, University of California; C. M. Bowra, *From Virgil to Milton*, 1945, Macmillan; *Heroic Poetry*, 1952, Macmillan; Ian Jack, *Augustan Satire*, 1952, Oxford University Press; E. M. W. Tillyard, *The English Epic and its Background*, 1954, Chatto; G. A. Wilkes, *The Thesis of Paradise Lost*, Melbourne University Press, 1961; B. A Wright, *Milton's Paradise Lost*, 1962, Methuen; A. D. Ferry, *Milton's Epic Voice*, 1963, Oxford University Press; J. S. Cunningmah, *Pope: The Rape of the Lock*, Arnold Studies in English Literature, 1970, E. Arnold; Paul Merchant, *The Epic*, 1971, Methuen; H. Erskine-Hill, *Pope: The Dunciad*, Arnold Studies in English Literature, E. Arnold, 1972.

Imagery

Very many literary critics talk about the imagery of this or that poem, play or novel as if the meaning of the term 'imagery' were universally agreed upon. This is not so. Some writers limit its application to figurative language: images for them are similes and metaphors. For example, Caroline Spurgeon, in her famous book on Shakespeare's imagery, uses the term 'image' as the best available one to cover every kind of simile, as well as every kind of metaphor (which she calls compressed simile). She asks her readers to divest their minds of the hint that the term carries of visual image only, and to think of it as 'connoting any and every imaginative picture or other experience, drawn in every kind of way, which may have come to the poet, not only through any of his senses, but through his mind and emotions as well, and which he uses, in the forms of simile and metaphor in their widest sense, for purposes of analogy' (*Shakespeare's Imagery and what it tells us*, 1935, p. 5). The 'imaginative picture' referred to here can obviously be extended to take up a large part of a scene (the imagery of the neglected garden in *Richard II*) or, at the other extreme, can be suggested by a single word (*'ripeness* is all': *King Lear*, V, ii, II).

A second use of the term 'imagery' is also quite common. Several critics employ it to include all the objects or qualities which make an impression on any of the five senses, and refuse to leave out of account the possibility that an image may be created by direct description as well as by means of simile and metaphor. C. D. Lewis calls a poetic image 'a picture made out of words', and goes on to suggest that 'an epithet, a metaphor, a simile may create an image; or an image may be presented to us in a phrase or passage on the face of it purely descriptive' (The Poetic image, 1965 edn., p. 18). If one understands the term in this broad sense, and applies it to Sonnet 65 of Shakespeare ('Since brass nor stone . . . '), then one will take the imagery of the poem to include the literal objects (brass stone, earth, sea) as well as the 'breath' of summer in line 5 and the 'siege of battering days' in line 6. In the same way, the imagery of Wordworth's sonnet

Upon Westminster Bridge would include the literal objects
(ships, towers, domes, theatres, temples) as well as the
metaphorical garment worn by the city.

In discussions of Shakespeare's plays, there is now a
pronounced tendency to extend the meaning of the term
'imagery' to include much more than rhetorical figures,
iterative words or even direct reference to objects. Those who
think of a Shakespeare play not primarily as words on a page
but as an imaginative experience which assumes its full
significance only in stage performance will naturally be conscious of that large body of non-verbal images which cannot
be found in the spoken words of the text but which are directly
presented in performance and function just as effectively as do
verbal images in forwarding the design. Examples might be
drawn from almost any of the plays: the properties and stage
effects associated with blood and noise in *Macbeth;* the storm
and its portents together with the sight of blood and fire in
Julius Caesar; the display of gold in *Timon of Athens;* the symbolic use of costume in *Coriolanus.* The most satisfying definition of Shakespearian dramatic imagery is one which takes
fully into account the fundamental differences between the
functions of the images in a lyric poem and those in a drama.
This distinction between poem and drama is of the utmost importance. Its critical implications are pointed out by R. A.
Foakes. 'While it is possible,' he remarks, 'for a poem to be a
metaphor, to exist only in an image or images, this cannot
properly be said of a Shakespearian play. The poetic image in
a play is set in a context not of words alone, but of words,
dramatic situation, interplay of character, stage-effect, and is
also placed in a time-sequence' (*Shakespeare Survey*, 5, 1952, pp.
85–6).

The commonest single type of image is the visual one, and
some writers tend to confine the term to the presentation of
visible objects and scenes. There is not really much point in
doing this. It is easy to find poems whose images arise from
senses other than that of sight, even though many of them
may also have a visual association. Tennyson's Song (*A Spirit
Haunts the Year's Last Hours*) is an example:

> The air is damp, and hushed and close,
> As a sick man's room when he taketh repose

An hour before death
My very heart faints and my whole soul grieves
At the moist rich smell of the rotting leaves . . .

There is an appeal here to touch and smell as well as to sight.
In his *Ode to Autumn*, Keats appeals to the ear when he writes
of 'the murmurous haunt of flies on summer eves', and strongly to taste when he talks of Autumn conspiring with the
maturing sun

To bend with apples the moss'd cottage trees
And fill all fruit with ripeness to the core
To swell the gourd and plump the hazel shell

While it is clear that images can be conveyed in non-figurative
language, it remains true that, as C. D. Lewis points out,
'trends come and go, diction alters, metrical fashions change,
even the elemental subject-matter may change almost out of
recognition; but metaphor remains, the life-principle of
poetry, the poet's chief test and glory' (*The Poetic Image*, p. 17).
Day Lewis is able to draw on the authority of Aristotle: 'The
greatest thing by far is to have a command of metaphor. This
alone cannot be imparted by another. It is the mark of
genius'. Shakespeare's unrivalled command of metaphor is
one of the major reasons for his pre-eminence as a lyric poet
and poetic dramatist.

In a general discussion of imagery, perhaps the most useful
distinction to be drawn is between poets who seem to think of
imagery as ornament, and those who use imagery organically,
adapting it to the structural and thematic conditions of poem
or play, giving it some real work to do in its context. The distinction between the two uses of imagery can be illustrated by
comparing Shakespeare's practice in his early plays with that
in his mature ones. In the earlier works, particularly the very
early comedies, images tend to appear for their own sake, and
not for anything they do: they are virtually independent of
any dramatic context. They are luxurious (though often
beautiful) digressions. As Shakespeare matures, his imagery
adapts itself more and more organically to the structure and
form of his plays. The relationship, for example, between his
images and the situations which give rise to them becomes

closer; the imagery becomes more suited to the character using it; imagery is more closely integrated with the theme and atmosphere of the play and the exigencies of the action.

The most striking feature of Shakespeare's greater plays (and of the greater sonnets) is the condensation and suggestiveness of the imagery, the compression into a short sentence or phrase of a whole range of associations. There are occasions, as W. Clemen points out, when 'the speed of the play, or of the scene, may not permit the development of the whole image, so that as a result, the image merely flashes up for a moment. . . . the insertion of a wholly-executed image would mean retarding and interrupting the rapid progress of the dramatic action' (*The Development of Shakespeare's Imagery,* 1951, p. 102). The growth in depth and concentration of Shakespeare's power of metaphorical expression may be illustrated by contrasting the speech of the sleepless Henry IV appealing to sleep and celebrating its benefits ('O sleep, O gentle sleep / Nature's soft nurse: *Henry IV,* Pt. II, III, i, 6ff) with Macbeth's speech on the same theme ('Methought I heard a voice cry Sleep no more . . . II, ii, 35). In King Henry's speech we have a leisurely, highly elaborate contemplation of the effects of sleep on various social classes spread over twenty-six lines. Macbeth compresses a similar contemplation into four lines, and what is more, these four lines are dramatically more appropriate than Henry's twenty-six. They are in no sense a digression: they dramatise a major preoccupation of the speaker and of the play.

The difference between 'ornamental' imagery whose main purpose is decorative effect (depending, to use F. R. Leavis's dismissive formula, 'on our being taken up in a kind of lyrical intoxication that shall speed us on in exalted thoughtlessness') and 'organic' imagery which is there to do something more than merely invite admiration might be illustrated by juxtaposing a celebrated piece from Tennyson with a Shakespeare sonnet:

(a)
  There is sweet music here that softer falls
  Than petals from blown roses on the grass,
  Or night-dews on still waters between walls
  Of shadowy granite, in a gleaming pass;

Music that gentlier on the spirit lies,
Than tired eyelids upon tired eyes;
Music that brings sweet sleep down from the blissful skies.
                    (from the *Choric Song of the Lotos-Eaters*)

(b)
Since brass, nor stone, nor earth, nor boundless sea,
But sad mortality o'ersways their power,
How with this rage, shall beauty hold a plea,
Whose action is no stronger than a flower?
O how shall summer's honey breath hold out
Against the wrackful siege of batt'ring days
                                                    (Sonnet 65)

It is clear that the poet of the first extract is taking justifiable pride in the beauty of his images, and offering them primarily for their decorative value. The movement of the lines is relaxed and leisurely; they are almost totally lacking in the density and richness of implication of the Shakespeare sonnet which is, by contrast, marked by feverish, almost bewildering, metaphorical activity.

In discussing the range of subjects from which imagery is drawn at given periods in literary history, we must take account of historical circumstances. It has often been remarked that Elizabethan lyric poets were much less adventurous in their choice of images than were the seventeenth-century Metaphysicals. But it should be remembered that much Elizabethan lyric verse was written for music. Some of the consequences of this are pointed out by C. D. Lewis: 'Bold, intense or closely-wrought images are inappropriate to verse written for music, since they tend to destroy the balance between the word-pattern and the melodic line. . . When words are written for tunes already existing or written in collaboration with a musician or written, as by the Elizabethans at a period when the lyric is thought of as a poem to be sung, the resulting poems tend to be subdued in their imagery and to seem shallow and even lifeless out of their original setting' (*The Poetic Image*, p. 49). For this reason, the divorce of lyric poetry from music (which the Metaphysical poets influenced and encouraged) had a profound effect on the extension of the scope and subject-matter of imagery. The new freedom enjoyed by the Metaphysicals has been compared to 'some gold-rush of half-inspired, half-demented prospectors, streaming out alike over the most homely, the most inaccessible, the most charming and the most forbidding regions of human experience in search for new veins of imagery'. Into the more successful Metaphysical poems we find compressed a great variety of images drawn from most unexpected sources, together with elaborate and ingenious parallels: Donne sees separated lovers as the two feet of a draughtsman's compass; Crashaw sees the weeping eyes of the Magdalene as 'portable and compendious oceans'. The Metaphysical extension of the field of imagery had a powerful influence on some twentieth-century poets: T. S. Eliot, Ezra Pound, Dylan Thomas, for example.

See separate article on Conceit, Metaphor and Simile.

Bibliography: H. W. Wells, *Poetic Imagery*, 1924, Milford; S. J. M. Brown, *The World of Imagery*, 1927, Keegan Paul; G. W. Knight, *The Wheel of Fire*, 1930, Oxford University Press; *The Imperial Theme*, 1931, Oxford University Press; C. Spurgeon, *Shakespeare Imagery and what it Tells Us*, 1935, Cambridge University Press; C. Brooks, *The Well Wrought Urn*, 1947, Harcourt Brace; R. Tuve, *Elizabethan and Metaphysical Imagery*, 1947, University of Chicago, also Cambridge Univeristy Prerss see under 'Conceit'; C. D. Lewis, *The Poetic Image*, 1947, Cape; R. B. Heilman, *This Great Stage: Image and Structure in King Lear*, 1948, Louisiana State University Press; W. Clemen, *The Development of Shakespeare's Imagery*, 1951, Methuen; T. R. Henn, *The Lonely Tower: Studies in the Poetry of W. B. Yeats*, 1965, Methuen; John Wain, ed., *Interpretations*, 1955, Routledge; C. B. Cox and A. L. Dyson, *Modern Poetry: Studies in Practical Criticism*, 1963, E. Arnold; C. B. Cox and A. E. Dyson, *The Practical Criticism of Poetry*, 1965, E. Arnold.

Inscape and Instress

Gerard Manley Hopkins (1844–89) is one of the most genuinely original of all English poets. His technical innovations and experiments in language, diction, metre and rhythm are unparalleled in the history of English poetry; he did so much that was totally new that he was obliged to invent a new terminology to describe his creative principles and technical procedures. It is important to realize that Hopkins's peculiar use of language is not the result of crass eccentricity or oddness: it derives from a deeply-held set of convictions about the nature of poetry and the poet's function. In order to understand his poetry, the reader must take account of the implications of two terms coined by Hopkins to describe his aims and methods. These terms are inscape and instress.

Hopkins coined the term inscape, which he nowhere explicitly defines, to describe the unified set of qualities in an object which inseparably belong to it, or are typical of it, so that through familiarily with these qualities we may grasp the individual essence of the object. Hopkins was passionately conscious of the importance of the distinctive individuality of everything from the most humble objects in creation to the mind of man, for him the most individual of all created things. (See the sonnet *That Nature is a Hericlitean Fire,* where man is seen as Nature's 'bonniest, dearest to her, her clearest-selved spark'). For Hopkins, each thing had its own inscape, its marked individuality or selfhood which expressed itself in some design or pattern. It was the poet's duty to observe things with the concentration necessary to grasp their uniqueness and so to inscape them. Hopkins' interest in the inscape or distinct individuality of all things had strongly religious overtones; the more conscious he became of the uniqueness of each object, the more deeply he was aware of its ultimate source; everything he inscaped seemed to him to throw off 'sparks that rang of God' (see *The Windhover*). As Hopkins used it, the term 'inscape' can be applied to a poet's work. He set out to express his own inscape, to give his readers an insight into the things which made him distinctive as a poet and as a man, to make his personality breathe through every line. Thus, what may appear to be eccentricity and mannerism, is really the expression of Hopkins' powerful individuality.

In order to express the inscapes or distinctive qualities of .things, Hopkins was forced to use language in an entirely new way. The inscape of every given object is, by definition, unique, so Hopkins was driven to the invention of new compound words in an attempt to express the essence of things as he contemplated them. This is the reason why we find so many apparently monstrous adjectival groups in front of nouns:

> selfwrung, selfstrung, sheathe- and shelterless thoughts
> > (*Spelt From Sibyl's Leaves*)

> the rolling level underneath him steady air
> > (*The Windhover*)

> the wimpled-water-dimpled, not-by-morning-matched face
> > (*The Golden Echo*)

> the widow-making unchilding unfathering deeps
> > (*The Wreck of the Deutschland*)

In *The Windhover*, Hopkins writes of the 'dapple-dawn-drawn Falcon'. Here he isolates one aspect of the bird to express what he thinks is its individual essence or inscape: for him, at the moment of writing, the essential thing about the falcon was that it was riding the dawn as if it were on a charger. Sometimes, the inscape of a thing can be expressed in a single word, e.g. 'the fell of dark' (in the sonnet 'I wake to feel the fell of dark not day'). The dark's inscape is found here in the terrifying qualities suggested by 'fell' (animal skin and malevolence). In *That Nature is a Hericlitean Fire,* Hopkins inscapes the dynamism of a cloudspace:

Cloud-puffball, torn tufts, tossed pillows flaunt forth, then chevy on an air-
built thoroughfare: heaven roysterers, in gay-gangs they throng; they glitter in marches.

A term related to inscape is instress, which for Hopkins means the force or energy which keeps a thing in existence and makes it strive after continued existence. Inscape stands for the inherent individuality of a thing, instress stands for the inherent energy or instinctive force which animates it. Hopkins could think of the instress of Nature as a divine energy that fills all things. The inscape can be perceived by the senses, and described in terms of physical impressions, but since the instress is a force, it must be expressed in terms of the impression an object makes on a person. To take an example, for Hopkins, an object displaying great activity often recalls the flames of fire; he also associates the sound of bells with the flames of fire. He thus expresses the instress of an object by associating different sense-impressions (i.e. by using the figure of speech known as synaesthesia: compare Dylan Thomas's 'tunes from chimneys' in *Fern Hill*). In *The Windhover*, we have the association of activity with the flames of fire and the pealing of bells to express the instress or distinctive force animating the falcon.

In a Meditation written about 1881, Hopkins declared: 'All things therefore are charged with love, are charged with God and if we know how to touch them give off sparks and take fire, yield drops and flow, ring and tell of him'. His sense of each natural thing vigorously asserting its inner identity is dramatically expressed in the following:

> As kingfishers catch fire, dragonflies draw flame;
> As tumbled over rim in roundy wells
> Stones ring; like each tucked string tells, each hung bell's
> Bow swung finds tongue to fling out broad its name;
> Each mortal thing does one thing and the same;
> Deals out that being indoors each one dwells;
> Selves – goes itself; myself it speaks and spells,
> Crying What I do is me: for that I came.

Bibliography: W. A. M. Peters, *G. M. Hopkins*, 1948, Oxford University Press; A. Heuser, *The Shaping Vision of G. M. Hopkins*, 1958, Oxford University Press; W. H. Gardner, *Gerald Manley Hopkins*, 2 vols, Oxford University Press, 1958; D. Davie, *Purity of Diction in English Verse*, 1967, Routledge; D. McChesney, *Hopkins Commentary*, 1968, University of London Press (i.e. Hodder).

Irony

Irony is one of the major tones of satire. The term derives from a Greek word meaning 'dissembler'. In Greek comedy, the dissembler was a character who assumed a false appearance, who pretended to be less intelligent than he was, who dealt in understatement, and who was able in these ways to triumph over his opposite, the fundamentally stupid, boastful character who tended to take things at their face value and was easily deceived. At the root of all irony is a contrast between what is being said, implied or suggested and what is actually the case. In every instance one is aware of the clever ironist or ironic observer on the one hand, and the unfortunate victim of the irony on the other. The ironist pretends to be unaware that the appearance is only an appearance; the victim of the irony is really unaware of the contrast between reality and appearance. A useful account is provided by Wayne Booth in his book *The Rhetoric of Irony*. Booth suggests that irony is present when the surface meaning of a passage must be rejected and another, incongruous and 'higher' meaning must be reached by reconstructing the evidence.

Much of the irony we find in poetry is verbal. In some cases of verbal irony, the speaker seems to be asserting one thing but wants the intelligent reader or listener to realize that he is really asserting something quite different. And the ironist is continually exercising his skill at the expense of some victim or other. If an intelligent speaker paid a glowing tribute to the generosity of somebody notorious for meanness, we should have to assume that he was being ironic. In such a case, the speaker is the *vehicle* of irony. A good example is found in *The Rape of the Lock*. Sir Plume makes a singularly unimpressive plea to the Baron for the return of Belinda's lock. The Baron's reply ('It grieves me much . . . who speaks so well should ever speak in vain': Canto IV, 131–2) is doubly ironic since (a) it is clear that the Baron is not at all grieved and (b) that Sir Plume has spoken far from well. Sometimes, however, the speaker is himself the *victim* of irony. Many poets use naive

speakers to put forward with perfect seriousness ideas which
the reader recognizes as absurd, ridiculous or otherwise objec-
tionable. The irony here lies in the contrast between the
speaker's erratic view of things and the knowing reader's ap-
preciation of their reality. In *Mac Flecknoe*, Dryden makes very
subtle ironic use of his speaker Flecknoe, who puts forward
the view that the man most fitted to succeed him as monarch
of the kingdom of nonsense is one like himself 'mature in
dulness from his tender years', and then goes on to nominate
Shadwell for the office as being the only one who 'stands confirm'd in full stupidity'. Here both the speaker and the person
spoken about are subjected to ironical contemplation.

There are some poems, *Mac Flecknoe* being one of them,
which depend for their whole point or impact on the continuous use of irony. One standard device is for the poet to assume the role of exaggerated admirer of something or
somebody he wants his readers to despise. The reader's enjoyment derives from his recognition of the contrasts between the
exaggerated tributes on the one hand, and the unpleasant
reality represented by those things to which they are paid, on
the other. A fine example of ironic eulogy is Swift's description of George II, a mediocrity incongruously cast in the role
of an eighteenth-century Augustus:

> Fair Britain, in thy Monarch blest,
> Whose Virtues bear the strictest Test;
> What Lineaments Divine we trace
> Through all his Figure, Mien and Face;
> Though Peace with Olive bind his hands
> Confest the conquering Hero stands. . .
>
>   (*On Poetry, A Rhapsody,* 1733)

This is paralleled by Pope in another ironic address to the
same monarch:

> To thee, the world its present homage pays,
> The harvest early, but mature the praise:
> Great friend of liberty! in kings a name
> Above all Greek, above all Roman fame:

Whose word is truth, as sacred and revered,
As Heaven's own oracles from altars heard.
Wonder of kings! like whom, to mortal eyes
None e'er has risen, and none e'er shall rise.

(*To Augustus*)

A prose version of the same technique is found in Book I of
Gulliver's Travels, which is a close allegory of English politics in
the early eighteenth century. Here is part of Swift's description of the Emperor of Lilliput: 'His features are strong and
masculine, with an Austrian lip and arched nose, his com-
plexion olive, his countenance erect, his body and limbs well
proportioned, all his motions graceful, and his deportment
majestic. He was then past his prime, being twenty-eight
years and three-quarters old, of which he had reigned about
seven, in great felicity, and generally victorious. . . . His voice
was shrill, but very clear and articulate, and I could distinctly
hear it when I stood up' (Book I, Chapter II). The irony of
this becomes plain only when the reader is aware that George
I, the target of Swift's satire at this point, was almost the exact
antithesis of the noble figure who governs the Lilliputians.
One commentator recalls 'George's thick and ungainly form,
his bad taste in dress, and his guttural and unintelligible
pronunciation of the little English he knew' (A. E. Case, *Personal and Political Satire in Gulliver's Travels,* 1945, p. 70).
    A common expedient of the ironist is to juxtapose two or
more contradictory, incongruous or incompatible objects,
statements, ideas or scenes. Pope does this quite often in *The
Rape of the Lock.* Consider the passage in which the world of the
bourgeoisie and the proletariat are incongruously juxtaposed
with that of the leisured class:

Mean while declining from the Noon of Day;
The Sun obliquely shoots his burning Ray;
The hungry Judges soon the sentence sign,
And Wretches hang, that Jury-men may Dine;
The Merchant from th' Exchange returns in Peace
And the long labours of the *Toilette* cease.

(Canto II, 19–24)

Here Pope provides a momentary glimpse of the real world which surrounds Belinda's artificial one. 'This momentary glimpse of the world of serious affairs, of the world of business and law, of the world of casualness and cruelty, is not introduced merely to shrivel the high concerns of polite society into ironical insignificance, though its effect, of course, is to mock at the seriousness with which the world of fashion takes its affairs. Nor is the ironical clash which is introduced by the passage uncalculated and unintentional: it is not that Pope himself is unconsciously callous – without sympathy for the "wretches". The truth is that Pope's own perspective is so scaled, his totality of view so honest, that he can afford to embellish his tempest in a teapot as lovingly as he likes without for a moment losing the sense of its final triviality' (Cleanth Brooks, *The Well Wrought Urn*, 1968 edn., pp. 83–4). Pope's ironical yoking together of the trivial and important gives rise to one of the characteristic figures of the poem, which is zeugma:

> Here Thou, Great *Anna*! whom three Realms obey,
> Dost sometimes Counsel take – and sometinmes *Tea*
> (Canto III, 7–8)

> When Husbands or when Lap-dogs breathe their last. . .
> (Canto III, 158)

> Or stain her Honour, or her new Brocade. . . .
> (Canto II, 107)

In *The Waste Land,* although Eliot is not confining himself to expressing anything so commonplace as the inferiority of the present to the past, we do find examples of the close juxtaposition of sordid modern scenes with glances at a more 'romantic' past. Much of the modern material is presented ironically: Madame Sosostris the clairvoyante, the rich neurotic lady, the Cockneys, Mrs. Porter, Mr. Eugenides, the typist and the carbuncular young man are distasteful figures. Against such unpleasing evocations of contemporary society Eliot sets representatives of more heroic times: Cleopatra, Elizabeth, Leicester, Ophelia. And yet to see the significance of the poem primarily in terms of a series of ironic contrasts between past and present is to read it superficially. Ophelia, for example, is not introduced merely as another memory of the golden past: her association with love and suffering identify her with both Philomel and the woman discussed by the two Cockneys. Eliot's main reason for introducing such a wide range of reference from many cultures and many ages was to make the reader aware not so much of contrasts as of resemblances. We are made to feel that the various waste lands glimpsed throughout the poem – biblical, classical, mediaeval and modern – are fundamentally alike.

Irony is a characteristic value of Shakespeare's mature work. The basic dramatic irony is that of a character taking an action which leads where he least expects it to. Examples of the operation of such irony are mentioned by R. B. Heilman: 'Othello, trying to punish an apparent wrong, commits a real wrong, much greater than the supposed one, and leaves himself infinitely worse off than if he had forgone the punitive satisfaction. A lesser irony . . . is that of circumstance, in which the human will operates minimally, or not at all: Cassio is the first person whose death is formally plotted, but he is the principal survivor' ('Modes of Irony in Othello', *Shakespeare's Tragedies,* ed. L. D. Lerner, 1964, p. 120). Other common instances of irony in drama are those in which a character speaks better than he knows, when he expresses truths one would not expect from him, when he makes statements which are true in a way that he cannot be conscious of, when he shows confidence in a future that the audience knows can only be bleak for him. Lady Macbeth tells her husband that his letters 'have transported me beyond / This ignorant present, and I feel now / The future in the instant' (I, v, 55). The irony here lies in the prosperous future she is contemplating, and the dire one the events of the play will unfold. She doesn't for a moment anticipate the horrors which her actual transformation beyond the 'ignorant present' (another irony) will actually involve. And King Duncan looks with admiration on the castle which is to be the scene of his murder, and hails his murderer as a benefactor.

Among English non-dramatic poets, the most extensive ironists are the great Augustan satirists, Dryden, Pope, Swift and Johnson. The destructive tone of Swift's irony may be

studied in a characteristic poem with the ironical title, 'A
Beautiful Young Nymph Going to Bed':

> Then seated on a three-legged chair
> Takes off her artificial Hair,
> Now, picking out a crystal Eye,
> She wipes it clean, and lays it by . . .

In a celebrated essay, F. R. Leavis declared that 'Swift's way
of demonstrating his superiority is to destroy, but he takes a
positive delight in his power . . . We have, then, in his writings
probably the most remarkable expression of negative feelings
and attitudes that literature can offer – the spectacle of
creative powers (the paradoxical description seems right) ex-
hibited consistently in negation and rejection' (The Irony of
Swift', in *The Common Pursuit*, 1962 edn., pp. 80 and 86).
Leavis is writing about Swift's prose, but finds his comments
on this equally applicable to the satiric verse.

Irony is not a characteristic mode of the Romantic poets,
Byron being the outstanding exception. A later poet whose
disenchanted view of life, and strong desire, as one of his
critics puts it, 'to expose human folly and humbug by ruth-
lessly stripping away all its pretensions', was Thomas Hardy.
A group of Hardy's poems, *Satires of Circumstance*, deal with unpleasant truths lurking beneath attractive surfaces. In one of
these, a young member of the congregation who 'adores' the
preacher for his spontaneity and freedom from affectation,
sees him

> re-enact at the vestry glass
> Each pulpit gesture in deft dumb-show
> That had moved the congregation so.

Some of Hardy's ironies are more bitter than this, as, for example, in *The Convergence of the Twain*, a poem inspired by the
loss of the *Titanic:*

> And as the smart ship grew
> In stature, grace and hue,
> In shadowy silent distance grew the iceberg too . . .

And here is his gloomy celebration of *Christmas 1923:*

> Peace upon the earth! was said. We sing it,
> And pay a million priests to bring it.
> After two thousand years of Mass
> We've got as far as poison gas.

In some influential modern discussions of poetry, irony is a most important critical term, since ironical overtones are often seen as being fundamental to mature literary work. In such accounts, irony is seen as a device for taking account of all the attitudes which threaten the one assumed by the poet in a particular poem. A successful poem is seen as one which does not simply put forward its author's convictions in easy generalities, but comes to terms with alternative convictions or emotions. David Daiches mentions an oversimplified example: 'If a poet can laugh at himself at the same time as he is being seriously passionate in a love-poem, he anticipates the possible laughter of others, and insures himself against parody. It is a kind of homeopathic treatment. The naive poet who does not, in his organization of images and his other poetic devices, take account of the waiting parodist or the potential mocker, will write a poem that slides too easily towards its meaning' (*Critical Approaches to Literature,* 1969, pp. 161–2). A contrast between two patriotic poems will help to illustrate what Daiches had in mind here. Yeats's *Easter 1916* is a successful patriotic poem. It does not present a discursive idea of patriotism; it does not ask approval for any one attitude or point of view; it does take account of mutually hostile ideas and emotions. It has nothing to offer the ironist, the parodist or the potential mocker. Yeats presents his materials with a degree of ambiguity which matches their complexity. The result is that the poem is able to survive what I. A. Richards has called 'ironical contemplation'. In it Yeats makes use of a special kind of irony: the bringing together of opposite, complementary impulses – approval and disapproval, delight and disappointment, a sense of terror and a sense of beauty.

A poem which, like *Easter 1916,* enacts its own ironies leaves little room for unfriendly readers to indulge in irony at its expense or that of its author. Much of the poetry of the seventeenth-century Metaphysicals belongs with the Yeats poem in this respect. On the other hand, there are very many poems which are unable to endure very much 'ironical contemplation'. Those which present limited experiences, emotions or attitudes in a straightforward, unqualified, single-minded way are obvious targets for the ironist or the parodist. Take as an example the following from another patriotic poem, this one by John Oxenham:

> He died as few men get the chance to die –
> Fighting to save a world's morality,
> He died the noblest death a man can die,
> Fighting for God, and Right and Liberty –
> And such a death is Immortality . . .

No account is taken here of the attitudes which threaten the ones expressed. Many patriotic poems, love poems, elegies and odes are extremely vulnerable to ironical contemplation, as are all poems which specialise in the expression of single emotions or aspirations: pride, ambition, admiration, optimism, sorrow or indignation. Poems such as this are easily overthrown by parody, which they invite.

Poets who show an ironical self-awareness, and maintain a balanced poise, insulate themselves from the unwelcome attentions of the ironist. Yeats's speakers often adopt a self-mocking stance, that of ironical observers of their own failings, as in *Among School Children:*

> And I though never of Ledean kind
> Had pretty plumage once – enough of that,
> Better to smile on all that smile, and show
> There is a comfortable kind of old scarecrow.

If one makes resistance to ironical contemplation and the possibility of parody a major criterion of poetic value, one is obliged to accord a relatively low place to much of the poetry of some periods (Romantic poetry, for example), and to examples of some poetic kinds: odes, elegies and patriotic effusions, for instance. This fact might well give rise to reservations about the absolute value of ironical contemplation as a critical touchstone. There is the further point that excessive fear of exposure to ironical contemplation has undoubtedly induced in many modern poets a neurotic dread of anything resembling a heroic stance. If the heroic note is sounded, it is often in mockery. The early work of T. S. Eliot has many examples.

The basis of irony as applied to language is, as G. N. Leech points out, "the human disposition to adopt a pose, or put on a mask. The notion of disguise is particularly pertinent, as it brings out (a) the element of concealment in irony, and (b) the fact that what is concealed is meant to be found out. If you dress up as a rabbit at a fancy-dress ball, you do not intend to be mistaken for a rabbit. In the same way, the mask of irony is not normally meant to deceive anyone – if it does, then it has the wrong effect. When someone takes an ironical remark at face value, we are justified in saying that he has 'failed to appreciate the irony' of it". (*A Linguistic Guide to English Poetry*, 1969, pp. 171–2).

Two other figures of speech are commonly associated with irony. These are hyperbole and litotes. Hyperbole is the figure which distorts the literal truth by overstating things, and is very extensively used by poets. A good example is found in Macbeth's horrified contemplation of his hands after he has murdered Duncan:

> What hands are here! Ha- they pluck out mine eyes!
> Will all great Neptune's ocean wash this blood
> Clean from my hand? No, this my hand will rather
> The multitudinous seas incarnadine,
> Making the green one red.
>
> (II, ii, 59).

Litotes, on the other hand, is the figure of understatement, in which an affirmative is expressed by the negative of its contrary. A celebrated instance of its use is St. Paul's 'I am a citizen of no mean city' (*Acts*, XXI, 39). The colloquial use of litotes is widespread, particularly to convey disparagement (He's no genius for 'he's stupid') or modesty (as when somebody who does something heroic declares that 'it was nothing'), or when the speaker feels too deeply to express himself in plain terms. The three terms, irony, hyperbole and litotes, have in common one significant feature: in none of them is the true state of things expressed: in the case of irony the speaker says or implies the opposite of what he knows to be true; hyperbole goes too far, and litotes understates. The effect of all three figures depends on the reader or listener being conscious of the reality from which the writer or speaker deviates for the sake of effect; those who use them do not mean to deceive. In order to succeed, irony, hyperbole and litotes must carry with them some indication that they are not to be taken at face value: the reader is induced to discover the 'true' interpretation by rejecting the literal one as inappropriate or impossible in the context.

See separate article on Satire.

Bibliography: J. A. K. Thomson, *Irony: An Historical Introduction*, 1926, Allen & Unwin; I. A. Richards, *Principles of Literary Criticism*, 1928, Harcourt Brace; A. R. Thompson, *The Dry Mock, Berkeley*, 1948, University of California; N. Frye, *Anatomy of Criticism*, 1957, Oxford University Press; N. Knox, *The Word Irony and its Context, 1500–1755*, 1961, Cambridge University Press; W. Booth, *The Rhetoric of Fiction*, 1961, University of Chicago; F. R. Leavis, *The Irony of Swift, in the Common Pursuit*, 1962, Chatto in association with Penguin; A. E. Dyson, *The Crazy Fabric: Essays in Irony*, 1965, Macmillan; D. C. Muecke, *The Compass of Irony*, 1969, Methuen; *Irony*, 1970, Methuen; Wayne Booth, *The Rhetoric of Irony*, 1974, University of Chicago.

Lyric

The traditional classification of poetry is into three kinds: narrative, dramatic and lyrical. But when one comes to examine individual poems, one often finds that many of them stubbornly resist simple description in terms of any one of these three. Few poems are purely narrative, dramatic or lyrical. *Paradise Lost,* being an epic, has large narrative elements, but it is also partly dramatic and partly lyrical. Wordsworth wrote poems called lyrical ballads. Some dramas (Eliot's *Murder in the Cathedral,* for example) contain lyrical passages. One can speak of dramatic and non-dramatic lyrics. A lyric poem has no fixed form: it may be an ode (an elaborated, exalted treatment of a serious subject), an elegy (generally a formal lament), or a sonnet, for example. Outside pure epic (narrative), or pure drama, almost all poetry is lyrical.

In general terms, it is its personal quality, its expression of individual thought and feeling, that gives lyrical poetry its character. Ruskin defined it as 'the expression by the poet of his own feelings'. A lyric is a non-narrative poem, featuring a single speaker, whose purpose is to share a state of mind, a mood or attitude with his reader. In a non-dramatic lyric, the speaker is a solitary figure (Shelley's *Ode to the West Wind,* his *Stanzas Written in Dejection,* for example). In a dramatic lyric, the speaker is placed in a concrete situation, and is speaking for the benefit of somebody else, whose presence in the poem is clearly implied. In Donne's *The Good Morrow* and *The Anniversarie,* a particular context is created for the speaker's address to his mistress. The dramatic monologue is a variety of lyric, since its main focus is on the character and personality of the speaker. Most of the great Romantic poems are lyrics, being largely taken up with the revelation of individual temperament, and recording, often in minute detail, spiritual histories, beliefs, feelings and moods.

It is a matter of extreme delicacy to differentiate between the 'I' (the speaker of the lyrical poem) and the poet. Sometimes we know a great deal about the life and thought of

a particular poet: Milton, Wordsworth, Keats and Shelley are
examples. When we find that some of the poems of these
authors seem to reflect what we know of their circumstances
and attitudes, we are naturally tempted to read such poems as
pure autobiography, and to say that the 'I' is simply the poet
speaking about himself. A classic example is Milton's sonnet
'When I consider how my light is spent'; another is
Wordsworth's *Tintern Abbey*. But even in such cases, it must be
emphasised that the poems are significant not because they
tell us what Milton and Wordsworth thought about their
chosen topics (although this is of great interest), but because
they express ideas and emotions which can be universally ap-
prehended. In such cases, it may be well to recall T. S. Eliot's
distinction between the man who suffers and the mind which
creates. A convenient critical device is the use of the term *persona* to describe the speaker in a lyrical or dramatic poem.
When we call the speaker of a poem a *persona* (or mask) we are
stressing the point that he is a fictitious character invented for
the purposes of a particular poem, and not a speaking likeness
of the poet. Even in such poems as *Lycidas*, which so many
readers have found so full of autobiographical implications,
Milton makes it clear that his speaker is such a persona. He is
the 'uncouth swain' who sings to the 'oaks and rills', not John
Milton, M.A. of Cambridge, although in much of what he
says he may be reflecting his creator's attitudes.

Is the speaker in a lyric poem ever identical with the poet?
To try to answer this question it is best to imagine all the
poems ever written placed on a scale, at one extreme end of
which are those (many of Donne's *Songs and Sonnets,* for example) in which the speaker is dramatically presented and
quite separate from the poet, and at the other those in which
everything we know and feel suggests a total identification
between speaker and poet, the speaker being the poet's
mouthpiece (Yeats's *Circus Animals' Desertion*). It has been
argued that 'the assumption and, therefore, the revelation of a
character other than the author's own is something which
Hardy rarely achieves – probably rarely even attempts' (Kenneth Marsden, *The Poems of Thomas Hardy, A Critical Introduction,* 19, pp. 94–5). Most of the poems we read would find a
place between the extremes of personality and impersonality.
The difficulty of knowing whether one is confronting the poet

himself or one of his masks is underlined in the following comments on Yeats's *Easter 1916:* "The 'I' is Yeats himself, for once a poet without a mask. Or is it Yeats wearing his bardic mask? Normally he is far too conscious of our kaleidoscopic roles as men to use an 'I' which is directly himself. In the Wordsworthian sense, he is the least 'personal' of our poets. But here, he makes a very near approach to the personal – possibly because the theme passionately attracted him, and the bardic role was very particularly his own" (C. B. Cox and A. E. Dyson, *Modern Poetry, Studies in Practical Criticism,* 1963, p. 59).

In its origins, lyrical poetry had intimate associations with music, hence its name. 'Lyrical' is often used as a term to describe all poetry which is, or can be imagined to be, sung to the accompaniment of a musical instrument. It is true that very many lyrical poems were composed with such an end in view. Much of the lyric verse of the Elizabethans (who thought of the lyric as a poem to be sung) was written for music, and almost all of it under strong musical influence, carefully preserving a proper balance between the word-pattern and the melodic line:

> Now winter nights enlarge
> The number of their hours
> And clouds their storms discharge
> Upon their airy flowers.
> Let now the chimneys blaze,
> And cups o'erflow with wine;
> Let well-tuned words amaze
> with harmony divine...
>
> Thomas Campion, *Two Books of Aires.*

In the Metaphysical poetry of the early seventeenth century, there is a striking tendency to divorce lyric poetry from music. The contrast between the fluency and smoothness of most Elizabethan lyrics or sonnets and the vivid, dramatic speech movements of Donne's *Songs and Sonnets,* for example, is remarkable. One cannot imagine Donne, so careless of verbal melody and fluid, easy movement, having written the great majority of his lyrics with a musical accompaniment in mind. They call for dramatic recitation, not singing.

One of the most popular forms of English lyric poetry for almost three centuries was the ode. This form was traditionally used to mark great public occasions, or to treat of serious and exalted themes. From the Renaissance to the eighteenth century it enjoyed enormous prestige, partly because of the universal reverence of poets for verse forms deriving from classical antiquity (the odes of the Greek Pindar and the Roman Horace were models for all later writers in the form), and partly because both Pindaric and Horatian forms allowed considerable scope for technical virtuosity and elevated utterance. Some of the most memorable English poems are odes: Milton's *On the Morning of Christ's Nativity*, a brilliant exercise in metrical dexterity; Marvell's great *Horatian Ode Upon Cromwell's Return from Ireland;* Dryden's two odes for St. Cecilia's Day; Gray's *Bard,* an exercise in the Pindaric form. Many of the best-known Romantic poems are odes: Wordsworth's *Intimations of Immortality;* Keats's five great odes; Shelley's *West Wind;* Coleridge's *Dejection.* Since the end of the Romantic age, the ode has progressively lost its prestige. No serious twentieth-century poet would contemplate writing a traditional ode: exalted, elevated treatment of subjects of high seriousness would automatically invite parody or perhaps even be regarded as parody, and expose the writer to accusations of insincerity or a damaging lack of self-awareness.

See separate article on irony.

Bibliography: E. Rhys, *Lyric Poetry,* 1913; H. J. C. Grierson, *Lyrical Poetry of the Nineteenth Century,* 1929; G. N. Schuster, *The English Ode from Milton to Keats,* 1940; C. M. Ing, *Elizabethan Lyrics,* 1951; J. L. Kinneavy, *A Study of Three Contemporary Theories of Lyric Poetry,* 1957; Carol Maddison, *Apollo and the Nine, A History of the Ode,* 1960; M. L. Rosenthal, *The Modern Poets,* 1960; *The New Poets,* 1967; Edwin Muir, *The Estate of Poetry,* 1962; John Heath-Stubbs, *The Ode,* 1969.

Metaphor and Simile

The Shorter Oxford Dictionary defines metaphor as 'the figure of speech in which a name or descriptive term is transferred to some object to which it is not properly applicable'. By 'properly' here the writer means 'literally'. A second dictionary definition helps to re-inforce the first one. A metaphor, according to Webster's New Collegiate Dictionary, is 'a word or phrase literally denoting one kind of object or idea used in place of another by way of suggesting a likeness or analogy between them'. Derivation helps to clarify meaning. 'Metaphor' is based on a combination of two Greek words meaning 'to carry over' or 'to carry across'. A term or expression is carried over from its common usage to another, uncommon, one, or some qualities or attributes of one object are carried over to another, in such a way that the second object is then referred to as if it were the first. All metaphors imply the recognition on the part of their user of some point of identity or comparison between normally unconnected objects. Metaphors range from the comparatively tame and unadventurous ('Life is a pilgrimage') through the apt and memorable ('When to the sessions of sweet silent thought / I summon up remembrance of things past') to the surprising and original ('Where can we find two beter hemispheres / Without sharp north, without declining west': Donne on two lovers) to the far-fetched ('these eyes and ears / Oft fed with true oathes, and with sweet salt tears') and even to the ludicrous, as in Crashaw's account of Mary Magdalen's eyes ('Two walking baths; two weeping motions / Portable and compendious oceans').

When they are examined, metaphors can be reudced to two elements: the subjects to which the metaphoric words refer (Magdalen's eyes in the final example above) and the metaphoric words themselves ('baths'; 'motions'; 'oceans'). The critic I. A. Richards devised the term *tenor* for the subject of a metaphoric word and the term *vehicle* for the metaphoric word itself. While it is unwise to multiply critical terms without clear justification, these are convenient terms which can save space in discussion. Metaphors are of three kinds: dead, dying (or weary or worn out) and living. A dead metaphor is one which can no longer evoke in the mind a picture of the imagery of its origin. Dead metaphors have been used so often that the writer as well as the reader (or speaker or hearer) have ceased to be aware that the words are not being used literally. Two examples of dead metaphors (metaphors which are dead for most readers, at any rate) are: 'The situation is now in hand' and 'he is carefully sifting the evidence'. Few people would recognize the original imagery from horsemanship in the first of these metaphors or call to mind a sieve in the case of the second. Those who use them almost always do so without intending to write figuratively.

Metaphors of the second kind (dying, weary, worn-out) are the least satisfactory of all. They are invariably regarded with contempt by discriminating judges of style. F. L. Lucas writes of 'weary old metaphors, decrepit with long years of service', which 'bring at each reappearance not pleasure but nausea'. George Orwell writes of 'a huge dump of worn-out metaphors which have lost all evocative power and are merely used because they save people the trouble of inventing phrases for themselves'. The following are familiar examples of worn out, dying metaphors: ring the changes on; take up the cudgels for; ride roughshod over; stand shoulder to shoulder with; fish in troubled waters; put our shoulder to the wheel; play into the hands of; the long arm of the law; saved at the eleventh hour. Examples might be multiplied.

A living or live metaphor is one that readily evokes a mental picture of the imagery of its origin. Living metaphors are offered with a full consciousness of their nature as substitutes for their literal equivalents. Consider the following two metaphors: (a) The wind howls; (b) The cold wind prowls round the windows. The first is a dead metaphor; it was once a living one, but has passed into common speech. The second is a living one, as is the following from *The Winter's Tale*, where Camillo, watching Florizel and Perdista (who is blushing) says 'He tells her something / That makes her blood look out' (IV, iv, 160).

The creation of metaphor is a traditional human habit, and something to which we do not normally advert is the fact that much of present-day language is built on the dead metaphors of our ancestors. One philologist has suggested that 'every expression that we employ, apart from those that are connected with the most rudimentary objects and actions, is a metaphor, though the original meaning is dulled by constant use' (see F. L. Lucas, *Style,* 1955, p. 165). The word 'metaphor' is itself a metaphor, though a dead one. Many people who speak of the 'eye of a needle' and the 'teeth of a saw' do not realize that they are using dead metaphors, nor do most of those who speak of others as being 'well off' realize that the expression may have had its origin in the metaphor of a ship safely away from the perils of the shore. Every language is largely a conglomeration of forgotten metaphors, and a study of the derivation of these can tell one a good deal about the social history and mentality of its original users. Latin, for example, was in its origin the language of a race of peasant soldiers. Many of its military terms were originally metaphors derived from agriculture (*agmen,* originally a driven line of animals, came to represent troops in a column; *cohors,* originally a cattle or sheep pen, became a company of soldiers; *acies,* a cutting edge, became a line of battle).

Metaphor can involve the user in some major infelicities of style. One common pitfall is the mixed metaphor, a subject which has long provided amusement at the expense of its unfortunate practitioners. A mixed metaphor occurs when two or more metaphoric words or expressions applied to the one subject are incongruous or incompatible with one another. The effects can often be ludicrous. A celebrated perpetrator of the hopelessly mixed metaphor was Sir Boyle Roche, member of Grattan's Parliament: 'Mr Speaker, Sir, I smell a rat; I see it floating in the air. But mark me, I shall nip it in the bud'. Members of the Irish Parliamentary Party at Westminster were similarly addicted: 'Now that the Minister has let the cat out of the bag, it is time to take the bull by the horns'. Mixed metaphor continues to flourish: 'All these bottlenecks and red tape must be ironed out'; 'We will not be swayed from our purpose by the red herrings with which our opponents are trying to cloud the issues'. Such lapses into mixed metaphor (where they are unconscious, and not contrived for amusement) come from a failure to visualise: the speakers do not really *see* what they are talking about. Users of mixed metaphor may be divided into two groups: those who mix their metaphors without being aware of the odd effects they are creating, and those who (like Shakespeare in his greater plays) mix their metaphors functionally, and thereby achieve a remarkable density of implication and suggestion.

Shakespeare's mixture of metaphors is of a different kind from that represented by the examples given above. Here is an instance from *Antony and Cleopatra*. The source of this play (North's translation of Plutarch's *Life of Marcus Antonius*) has the following comment on Antony's response to his betrayal by his former allies: 'When Antonius saw that his men did forsake him and yielded unto Caesar, and that his footmen were broken and overthrown, he then fled into the city, crying out that Cleopatra had betrayed him unto them with whom he had made war for her sake' (*Shakespeare's Plutarch*, ed. T. J. B. Spencer, 1964, p. 276). Here is how Shakespeare transforms his original:

> The hearts
>   That spaniel'd me at heels, to whom I gave
>   Their wishes, do discandy, melt their sweets
>   On blossoming Caesar: and this pine is bark'd
>   That overtopped them all. Betray'd I am
>   O this foul soul of Egypt! This grave charm,
>   Whose eyes beck'd forth my wars, and call'd them home;
>   Whose bosom was my crownet, my chief end,
>   Like a right gipsy, that at fast and loose
>   Beguil'd me, to the very heart of loss.
>
> (Iv, xii, 20ff).

Two features of this speech call for comment. One is that the chief difference between Antony's speech and the source is that Shakespeare has, through an abundant use of striking metaphor, vastly enriched what he has borrowed (his original is almost totally free of metaphor). The other is that while from one point of view some of the metaphors are inextricably mixed (hearts are spaniels which seem to melt as if they were sweets on a blossoming tree), from another the effect is to suggest vivid compression rather than confusion. One uncompleted metaphor tumbles out after another because the impatient speaker cannot control the tumultuous surge of his feelings. The turbulence and lack of easy logical progression from one metaphor to the next is altogether appropriate to the dramatic context. The same telescoping of metaphors is found in Lady Macbeth's

> Was the hope drunk
> Wherein you dress'd yourself? Hath it slept since?
> And wakes it now to look so green and pale
> At what it did so freely?
>
> (I, vii, 35-8)

Metaphor, along with simile, is the writer's chief mode of achieving concreteness and vitality. By means of a successful metaphor, he gains strength and clarity of impression. A vivid metaphor can impress its meaning more memorably and more indelibly than almost any passage of abstract discourse, however well written. The concrete image created by the compelling metaphor must inevitably be more telling than any set of· abstractions. The superiority of Shakespeare's densely metaphorical passage in *Antony and Cleopatra* to its relatively abstract and literal source in North's *Plutarch* has already been noted. The superiority of the vivid metaphor to any literal equivalent becomes clear when one tries to provide literal paraphrase for lines such as the following:

> O how shall Summer's honey breath hold out
> Against the wrackful siege of batt'ring days. . . .
>
> (Shakespeare, Sonnet 65)

> Three April perfumes in three hot Junes burned
> Since first I saw you fresh which yet art green
>
> (Shakespeare, Sonnet 104)

Johnson's comment to Boswell is apt: 'And Sir, as to metaphorical expression, that is a great excellence in style, when it is used with propriety, for it gives you two ideas for one: conveys the meaning more luminously, and generally with a perception of delight'. For Johnson himself, 'used with propriety' is the operative phrase here. He found much of the metaphorical expression of the Metaphysical poets (the conceits which twentieth-century readers have been taught to admire) far from proper. In their work, he declared, 'the most heterogeneous ideas are yoked by violence together; nature and art are ransacked for illustrations, comparisons and allusions; their learning instructs, and their subtlety surprises;

but the reader commonly thinks his improvement dearly bought, and though he sometimes admires, is seldom pleased' (*Life of Cowley*).

In most accounts of the subject, simile is regarded as a version of metaphor. Each figure involves a transference or carrying over of an aspect or aspects of one object to another object. In the case of each the making of a comparison is the fundamental point, but in the case of the simile, the comparison is openly proclaimed as such, whereas in the case of metaphor the comparison is implied. When Shakespeare writes 'Like as the waves make toward the pebbled shore / So do our minutes hasten to their end', he is using a simile; when he writes 'When to the sessions of sweet silent thought / I summon up remembrance of things past' he is using a metaphor. It is clear from these two examples that metaphor is capable of a greater range of suggestiveness than simile, that its implications are wider and richer. The simile, by its very nature (the 'like as . . . so do' formula), is limited to a comparatively small area of suggestion.

In his *Rhetoric,* Aristotle suggested that the simile is a metaphor with an explanation. Every metaphor presupposes a simile, and every simile may be compressed into a metaphor. The following metaphor from R. B. Sheridan's *School for Scandal* will illustrate this. Sir Benjamin Backbite is going to publish some love elegies on beautiful quarto pages, 'where a neat rivulet of text shall meander through a meadow of margin'. Had Sheridan written: 'The text will be found between wide margins like a rivulet in a broad meadow', he would have been using a simile. The metaphor actually used is much more striking than any alternative simile based on the same elements. The subjects of the metaphoric words (text and margin), and the metaphoric words themselves (rivulet and meadow) become so fused in the mind that one ceases to be conscious of the distinction between them. In the case of the simile, although a comparison is made, one is conscious of the differences between the objects, their separateness; one thinks of the simile as an exercise in make-believe, as if the writer were saying, 'Let's imagine for a moment that a text is like a rivulet and a margin like a meadow'. Most metaphors exist for the practical purpose of presenting a notion in an arresting or illuminating way, and in that sense they are highly functional. Many similes, on the other hand, particularly long ones, are used not primarily to illuminate but for their own sake, as opportunities to be seized to enhance the beauty of a passage, or to indulge a taste for ambitious descriptive effects, in which case they become digressions having little organic connection with the poem. Consider the following extended simile from Arnold's *Sohrab and Rustum*. At times one loses sight of its purpose as one luxuriates with the poet in his fine images:

> As when some hunter in the spring hath found
> A breeding eagle sitting on her nest,
> Upon the craggy isle of a hill lake,
> And pierced her with an arrow as she rose,
> And followed her to find out where she fell
> Far off – anon her mate comes winging back
> From hunting, and a great way off descries
> His huddling young left sole; at that, he checks
> His pinion, and with short uneasy sweeps
> Circles above his eyry, with loud screams
> Chiding his mate back to her nest; but she
> Lies dying, with the arrow in her side,
> In some far stony gorge out of his ken
> A heap of fluttering feathers: never more
> Shall the lake glass her, flying over it;
> Never the black and dripping precipices
> Echo her stormy scream as she sails by –
> So that poor bird flies home, nor knows his loss –
> So Rustum knew not his own loss, but stood
> Over his dying son, and knew him not.

(556ff)

Not all extended similes function like this one. In *Paradise Lost*, Milton makes use of a great number of extended epic similes, but these earn their place in the poem on practical grounds. They are, like Arnold's simile, ornamental, but they also answer the demands of Milton's narrative. Most of them are used to portray supernatural beings, their dwelling-places and their activities. The free use of epic simile is one of Milton's most effective methods of presenting the unknown in terms of the known, the inconceivable in terms of what may be conceived. They also contribute to the effects of strangeness and sublimity demanded by the theme of *Paradise Lost,* and are appropriate vehicles for the wide range of reference demanded by the epic genre.

In discussion of metaphor, two other figures should be mentioned: synedoche and metonymy. It has already been pointed out that metaphor involves tranference or carrying over of meaning from one word to another, on the ground that some resemblance is perceived between the objects represented by the words. Synedoche is a term used to describe a certain kind of transference: the use of the name for a part of something when the whole is meant. A famous example is Milton's use of 'blind mouths' for the Anglican clergy. Poets frequently use such expressions as 'a fleet of fifty sail' for fifty ships, and employers speak of workmen as 'hands'. Another term whose effect depends on transference is metonymy, defined in Webster's Dictionary as 'a figure of speech that consists in using the name of one thing for that of something else with which it is associated'. Metonymy is found in common speech ('The whole town rejoiced'; 'Do you like Shakespeare?' – the people of the town and works of Shakespeare being in question), and by poets of all ages. The following lines from Shirley's *Death the Leveller* provide a celebrated example:

> Sceptre and Crown must tumble down
> And in the dust be equal made
> With the poor crooked Scythe and Spade.

See separate article on Imagery.

Bibliography: J. M. Murray, *The Problem of Style,* 1922, Milford; *Countries of the Mind, Second Series,* 1931, Oxford University Press; C. Day Lewis, *The Poetic Image,* 1947, Cape: Isabel C. Hungerland, *Poetic Discourse,* 1958, University of California Press; L. C. Knights and B. Cottle, ed., *Metaphor and Symbol,* 1960, Butterworth (for Colston Research Society); W. Nowottny, *The Language Poets Use,* 1962, Athlone Press; Max Black, *Models and Metaphors,* 1962, Cornell University Press; T. Hawkes, *Metaphor,* 1972, Methuen; R. Wellek and A. Warren, *Theory of Literature,* 1963, Penguin; G. N. Leech, *A Linguistic Guide to English Poetry,* 1969, Longman.

Metaphysical Poetry

Since Samuel Johnson's discussion of their work in his *Lives of the English Poets,* it has been customary to describe Donne, Herbert, Crashaw, Vaughan and Marvell (to mention only the greater figures) as the English Metaphysical poets. In his *Life of Cowley* (1779) Johnson observed that 'about the beginning of the seventeenth century appeared a race of writers that may be termed the Metaphysical poets'. Johnson appears to have owed his use of the term to Dryden, who in 1693 complained that Donne 'affects the metaphysics, not only in his satires, where nature only should reign, but perplexes the minds of the fair sex with nice speculations of philosophy'. The term is not really a satisfactory one as applied to the poets mentioned above, since it suggests a poetry that has, in the words of H. J. C. Grierson, 'been inspired by a philosophical conception of the universe and the role assigned to the human spirit in the great drama of existence'. None of the seventeenth-century Metaphysical poets speculates in this large way about ultimate issues; they are interested in ideas chiefly for the witty and ingenious use they can make of these:

> At the round earth's imagined corners blow
> Your trumpets, angels, and arise, arise,
> From death, you numberless infinities
> Of souls, and to your scattered bodies go;
> All whom the flood did, and fire shall o'erthrow . . .
> (Donne, *Holy Sonnet* VII)

It is common to find Herbert, Vaughan, Marvell and the rest referred to as poets of the school of Donne or poets in the Donne tradition. This can be misleading if it is taken to mean that they were uninspired imitators or lacked individual talents, whereas each of them is, in his best work, unmistakably himself. Nevertheless to give an account of some of the major features of Donne's poetry is a convenient method of describing the outstanding characteristics of Metaphysical poetry.

One of the most remarkable things about Donne's poems is the extent to which they are taken up with arguments or attempts to persuade. In a way, all of his poems are exercises in the use and abuse of logic. A good illustration will be found in the final three lines of *The Good-Morrow*, which embody a syllogism or formal logical argument:

> Whatever dies, was not mix'd equally;
> If our two loves be one, or thou and I
> Love so alike that none can slacken, none can die.

In his love poems, he argues constantly with the object of his addresses, trying to persuade her to share this or that point of view; in the religious poems he cannot refrain from arguing with God, to Whom he addresses some outrageously witty paradoxes:

> That I may rise, and stand, o'erthrow me, and bend
> Your force, to break, blow, burn, and make me new . . .
>
> *(Holy Sonnet* XIV)

Then there is the vividly dramatic quality of Donne's poetry, much of which deals vividly and immediately with actual or imaginary experiences, situations and attitudes. Notice the dramatic opening of *The Good-Morrow*, particularly the position of the verb 'Did' at the beginning of the second line (Compare the effect produced by the carrying over of meaning from one line to another in the sonnet 'Batter my heart'). The vivid, often startling openings are one aspect of Donne's dramatic manner. Others are the reader's sense of a situation, a speaker and someone being spoken to. As we read Donne's love-poems and many of the sonnets, we have, more distinctly than in the case of almost any other poet, the impression of a living voice speaking from the page to us. The rhythms of Donne's verse are closer to those of the living, colloquial speech found in Shakespeare's greatest plays than to those of most lyrical poems. Many of Donne's poems are like performances by an actor enormously enjoying his brilliant displays of showmanship and virtuosity. The dramatic gifts displayed in the poems make it easy to understand why he was regarded as the greatest preacher of his age.

Donne is consistently witty, even in his very serious poems. Wit, arguably the essential feature of all Metaphysical poetry, implies quickness of intellect, the ability to say brilliant or sparkling things, to surprise and delight by means of unexpected thoughts or expressions. Donne's wit finds an outlet in paradoxes, puns and, above all, in conceits. A paradox is a statement which on the surface seems self-contradictory, but which turns out, on closer examination, to have a valid meaning, a meaning which goes beyond the bounds of common sense and logic. The sonnet "Batter my heart" is built around a series of powerful paradoxes. A concentrated paradox can be made by combining two words which in normal circumstances would not be found together (Wordsworth's 'aching joys' in *Tintern Abbey;* Milton's 'blind mouths' in *Lycidas*). A pun is a play on words identical in sound but quite different in meaning ('Donne' and 'done' in *A Hymn to God the Father,* a poem whose effect depends on skilful punning). A conceit is a comparison, often extended, between things which at first sight seem to have little or nothing in common (For a more detailed discussion of the conceit see the separate article on the subject). Those who do not like Donne's conceits tend to describe the comparisons they involve as far-fetched (see the comparison between lovers and hemispheres in *The Good-Morrow*). Johnson claimed that in the metaphysical conceit 'the most heterogeneous ideas are yoked by violence together'. Those who admire the conceit, on the other hand, stress the ingenuity, boldness and originality of the best examples. An example of the modern influence of the Metaphysical conceit will be found in the first few lines of T. S. Eliot's *Prufrock,* where the quiet evening is compared to a patient etherised upon a table.

A fact of major importance about Donne is that he greatly extended the scope and subject-matter of poetic imagery. He takes his images from a very wide range of subjects. The furniture of his love-poems is not limited to the assortment of stock properties traditionally employed by love-poets: gardens, balconies, nightingales and so on. His stimulates (or puzzles) the mind of his beloved with an impressively daunting array of images drawn from learned sources. Some of his most famous conceits are theological, medical, scientific, or drawn from geographical discovery and exploration, or the law, or mediaeval philosophy. The images in his divine poems are similarly wide-ranging:

> Let man's soul be a sphere, and then, in this,
> The intelligence that moves, devotion is,
> And as the other spheres, by being grown
> Subject to foreign motions, lose their own,
> And being by others hurried every day,
> Scarce in a year their natural forms obey . . .
>
> (*Good Friday, 1613, Riding Westward*)

But learned images are balanced by others which are homely and realistic:

> For God's sake hold your tongue, and let me love,
>   Or chide my palsy, or my gout,
> My five grey hairs, or ruined fortune flout . . .
>
> (*The Canonization*)
>
> I wonder by my troth, what thou, and I
>   Did, till we loved? were we not weaned till then,
> But sucked on country pleasures, childisly?
> Or snorted we in the seven sleepers' den?
>
> (*The Good-Morrow*)

Finally, Donne introduced a new tone into English love-poetry. The Elizabethan love-poet idealized the beloved, presented her as a paragon of beauty and virtue to be thought and spoken of with reverence. Donne's love-poetry can be impudent and insolent, sceptical and mocking, cynical and flippant; it is seldom idealistic, tender or reverential. His speakers think of the women they address as people who can respond to witty arguments and who might enjoy elaborate fooling or outrageous paradoxes. Dryden must have spoken for many puzzled readers when he declared that Donne 'perplexes the minds of the fair sex with nice speculations of philosophy, when he should engage their hearts, and entertain them with the softness of love'.

There are wide differences in style, tone, attitude and personality between the Metaphysical poets. Herbert is quieter, less tough-minded, less adventurous, less sophisticated than Donne, less troubled in his religious attitudes, quainter and more homely in his imagery, plainer and simpler in style; all his poetry is religious, and almost all of it spiritual autobiography. Marvell is more poised and urbane than either Donne or Herbert, relies much more on visual imagery than they do, and is fond of classical mythology, which the others tend to avoid. But all three have characteristic features in common which are more significant than these differences. The structure of their poems is normally dialectic; they make passionate arguments out of abstract ideas; their best poems have a logical structure, developing along the lines of a formal argument. This is so pronounced a feature that the 'arguments' of many of the poems can be reduced to a neat syllogistic formula. An extreme case is Marvell's *To His Coy Mistress,* whose argument can be expressed as folows: 'If we had endless time, I should not mind your coyness. But time is limited, therefore, in order to enjoy life, we must seize the fleeting moment'. The most interesting Metaphysical poems are those in which the reader is surprised by ingenious comparison and analogy between apparently unrelated subjects. All the Metaphysical poets have in common a fondness for tracing far-reaching correspondences between various levels of creation. This tendency is well summed-up in Marvell's lines in *The Garden,* where he talks of the mind as 'that ocean where each kind / Does straight its own resemblance find', all species on land having their counterparts in the sea. It is this tireless search for correspondences that finds an outlet in the metaphysical conceit, the charactertistic figure of Metaphysical poetry.

See separate article on Conceit.

Bibliography: George Williamson, *The Donne Tradition*, 1930, Oxford University Press; T. S. Eliot, *Selected Essays 1917–32*, 1932, Faber; H. J. C. Grierson, *The Metaphysical Poets in the Background of English Literature*, 1934, Chatto; F. R. Leavis, *Revaluation*, 1936, Chatto; H. C. White, *The Metaphysical Poets*, 1936, Macmillan; C. Brooks, *Modern Poetry and the Tradition*, 1939, Oxford University Press; B. Ford, ed., *From Donne to Marvell*, 1956, i.e. *Vol. 3 of 'Pelican Guide to English Literature'*, Penguin; J. B. Leishman, *The Monarch of Wit*, 1969, Hutchinson; *The Art of Marvell's Poetry*, 1966, Hutchinson; A. Alvarez, *The School of Donne*, 1961, Chatto; L. Unger, *Donne's Poetry and Modern Criticism*, 1962, Russell and Russell; H. Gardner, ed., *John Donne: A Collection of Critical Essays*, 1962, Prentice-Hall; Joan Bennett, *Five Metaphysical Poets*, 1964, Cambridge University Press; J. Winny, *A Preface to John Donne*, 1970, Longmans; M. Bradbury and D. Palmer, eds., *Metaphysical Poetry: Stratford-upon-Avon Studies, II*, 1970, E. Arnold.

Neo-classic and Romantic

These terms are used in a variety of ways in relation to English literature. Literary historians find in them convenient (even indispensable) labels for periods of English literary history, neo-classic (or Augustan) poetry being generally thought of as that written between the Restoration of 1660 and the decade or so preceding the French Revolution of 1789, and the first great landmark of the Romantic movement being Wordsworth's *Lyrical Ballads* (1798). The major Romantic poets, apart from Wordsworth and Coleridge, are Blake, Shelley, Keats and Byron, all of whom were dead by 1827. The use of 'neo-classic' and 'romantic' to describe fixed historical periods is, however, quite arbitrary, since recognizably 'classical' poetry was being written at the beginning of the seventeenth century by Ben Jonson, while convincing arguments have been advanced to suggest that there was a romantic revival in the middle of the eighteenth century. 'Romantic' poets still flourish. The general confusion about an acceptable meaning for romantic and romanticism is illustrated in the contrasting view of two influential modern critics. Northrop Frye sees Romanticism as a 'historic centre of gravity, which falls somewhere around the 1790–1830 period', while in a well-known book Frank Kermode uses the term as 'applicable to the literature of one epoch beginning in the late years of the eighteenth century and not yet finished, and as referring to the high valuation placed during this period upon the image-making powers of the mind at the expense of its rational powers' (*Romantic Image,* 1957, p. 56).

There are many people who think of neo-classic and romantic as terms standing for ideas rather than fixed periods, as representing the great polar opposites of English poetry, irrespective of dates, literary movements or eras. Most critics, however, prefer to limit the application of the terms to specific periods, in the belief that it is possible to isolate some major aspects of the theory and practice of neo-classic poetry (as exemplified in the work of Dryden, Pope and Johnson, for example) which set that poetry in sharp and essential contrast to that of the two generations of Romantic poets. René Wellek, for instance, argues that 'if we examine the characteristics of the literature we call romantic we find throughout the same conceptions of poetry and of the workings of nature and its relation to man, and basically the same poetic style, with a use of imagery, symbolism and myth which is clearly distinct from that of eighteenth-century neo-classicism'. Wellek isolates three main romantic criteria: 'imagination for the view of poetry, nature for the view of the world, and symbol and myth for poetic style' (*Concepts of Criticism*, 1963, p. 161).

One of the chief preoccupations of the neo-classic poets and critics was with man's activity as a social being, his duties and responsibilities as a member of an organized community. For them, town life represented the civilised ideal; two key Augustan words, 'politeness' and 'urbanity', underline the identification by neo-classic writers of civilisation with the town. They tended to fix their attention on the practical concerns of communal life, on social and public affairs, on the literary and artistic standards they thought appropriate to civilised man. Their greatest representatives stood for good order, moderation and reasonableness, a sense of responsibility to the society to which men owed so much. Their strongest feelings were most often aroused by those who violated the accepted norms of their society and threatened its balance. It is therefore not surprising that the most memorable poems of the neo-classic age are satires on those who would not follow reason, who seemed bent on destroying order and harmony in life and art, whose manners rendered them unfit members of polite society. Neo-classic poets constantly stress the need for man to recognise his limitations, not to aspire beyond his reach or entertain exaggerated ambitions. As Pope puts it,

> Know then thyself, presume not God to scan;
> The proper study of Mankind is Man.
> > (*Essay on Man*, Epistle II, lines 1–2)

The Augustan heroic or closed couplet, that most restrictive of verse forms, typifies the neo-classic acceptance of all kinds of limitation.

The great neo-classic poets were fundamentally conservative and traditionalist. This is not surprising in an age which feels that it has achieved a high degree of civilisation, and dreads above all things a relapse into barbarism. From Dryden to Johnson, poets revered and imitated the masters of classical antiquity, the translation and paraphrase of whose works was a universal practice. This discipleship gave the Augustans an easy command of a wide range of literary forms and fostered the virtues of conciseness, balance, elegance and craftsmanship. Against this, one must set their limitations. Devotion to the classical masters often involved a rigid adherence to 'rules'; the passion for 'correctness' could all too readily issue in lifeless, mechanical verse. One Romantic reaction is that of Keats, vigorous if exaggerated:

> Beauty was awake!
> Why were ye not awake? But ye were dead
> To things ye knew not of – were closely wed
> To musty laws lined out with wretched rule
> And compass vile. . . .
> Easy was the task:
> A thousand handicraftsmen wore the mask
> Of poesy. . . .
> *(Sleep and Poetry)*

The 'limited' subject-matter of Augustan poetry, together with its 'limited' range of styles and attitudes, inspired numerous unfavourable contrasts with the work of the great Romantics. The most extreme critical statement of the anti-Augustan case is that of Matthew Arnold, who wrote of Dryden and Pope as founder and high-priest respectively of 'our age of prose and reason', but who declared their work lacking in 'poetic largeness, freedom and insight'. In a famous pronouncement, Arnold claimed that 'the difference between genuine poetry and the poetry of Dryden, Pope and all their school, is briefly this: their poetry is conceived and composed in their wits; genuine poetry is conceived and composed in the soul'. This is question-begging, but it does isolate the stress in Augustan poetry on wit and the play of intellect rather than on the higher flights of imagination.

Some useful distinctions can be drawn between neo-classic and Romantic theory and practice in poetry. If the central concern of neo-classic writers was with man as a social being, a vital impetus behind the Romantic movement was the notion of individualism. A recurring topic of Romantic poetry is either the poet himself or some idealized version of him. The Augustan poet is concerned with the significance of human relationships; many of the memorable moments and situations of Romantic poetry feature isolated figures, even outcasts from society:

> Some might lament that I were cold,
> As I, when this sweet day is gone,
> Which my lost heart, too soon grown old,
> Insults with this untimely moan;
> They might lament – for I am one
> Whom men love not. . . .
> (Shelley, *Stanzas Written in Dejection*)

> Forlorn! The very word is like a bell
> To toll me back from thee to my sole self!
> (Keats, *Ode to a Nightingale*)

Examples might be multiplied. Romantic poets tend to find their inspiration in the solitary contemplation of non-human natural objects, and to project on to these their own hopes, fears, ideas and fantasies. The world chiefly explored by the Romantic poets was not the world of man in his social aspect but of the inner self. Of mountains, Dr Johnson remarked: 'I deny any grandeur to the spectacle. There is more emotion for me in a furlong of Cheapside than in the contemplation of more elevated bodies'. For the Romantics, on the other hand, mountains, winds, clouds, oceans, nightingales, albatrosses and other phenomena of wild nature took on a vast significance: they became symbols for the poets' states of mind; they often saw themselves in an active symbolic relationship with them (Shelley's west wind and his skylark, Keats's nightingale, for example). One of the great Romantic ideals was the liberation of the emotions and the imagination. The 'uncontrollable' west wind is an impressive symbol of this process.

All this, of course, involved a revolt against traditional forms and attitudes in poetry and criticism. The Romantics tended to find the neo-classic concern for traditional precedents and ancient rules impossibly limiting. When Augustan poets wrote 'serious' poetry they generally dealt with exalted subjects in exalted language; the Romantics made serious, even tragic, poems from humble, familiar material using common language. When even the most 'inspired' Augustans surveyed the human scene, they did so as rational, intelligent observers; in the hands of Wordsworth, Blake and Shelley, poetry became, in the words of the last-named, 'the trumpet of a prophecy', a medium for visions and dreams. Many Romantic poets found the role of prophet quite congenial. In his *Defence of Poetry*, Shelley makes claims for the poet and for poetry which no Augustan poet would have dreamed of making. Then again, Wordsworth's account of poetry as 'the spontaneous overflow of powerful feelings' is very far indeed from the neo-classic notion that poetry was an art to to be learned and mastered. And whereas the Augustans had been prepared cheerfully to set limits to the aims and expectations of poetry, the true Romantics could only think of the infinite possibilities open to the artist: he could even, as Shelley saw him, be an active agent in the regeneration of mankind.

An essential classical/romantic distinction is that between two metaphors of mind, which express two opposing views of the imagination. The first sees the mind as a reflector of external objects; the second as a projector or lamp, contributing to the object it perceives. The popular eighteenth-century view of the perceiving mind was as a passive receiver of fully-formed images, a mirror which accurately fixes the objects it reflects. M. H. Abrams points out that 'the analogies for the mind in the writings of both Wordsworth and Coleridge show a radical transformation of the eighteenth-century one.' The Romantics 'picture the mind in perception as active rather than inertly receptive, and contributing to the world in the very process of perceiving the world' (*The Mirror and the Lamp*, 1958 edn., pp. 57–69). One of Wordsworth's favourite analogies for the activity of the perceiving mind is that of a lamp projecting light. In *The Prelude,* he recalls that

>   an auxiliar light
> Came from my mind, which on the setting sun
> Bestow'd new splendour
>
>   (II, 378ff)

In *Tintern Abbey* we have the suggestion that the content of perception is, as M. H. Abrams glosses it, 'the joint product of external data and of mind'. The passage in question is that where Wordsworth speaks of

> all the mighty world
> Of eye and ear – both what they half create
> And what perceive. . . .

And towards the end of the *Immortality Ode,* Wordsworth affirms that

> The clouds that gather round the setting sun
> Do take a sober colouring from an eye
> That hath kept watch o'er man's mortality. . .

The transforming power of the Romantic imagination is colourfully suggested by William Blake: 'When the Sun rises, do you not see a round disc of fire somewhat like a guinea? O no, no. I see an innumerable company of the Heavenly host crying, Holy, Holy, Holy is the Lord God Almighty' (*Vision of the Last Judgement*).

Most attempts to isolate the essence of Romanticism concentrate on Romantic theories of the imagination. In this respect, the great poets of the English Romantic period form a coherent group. For none of them is the imagination merely the power of visualisation or even the inventive power. It is a creative power by which the mind, as I. A. Richards puts it, 'gains insight into reality, reads nature as a symbol of something behind or within nature not ordinarily perceived' (*Coleridge on Imagination*, 1934, p. 145). Here is how Blake expresses the idea·

> To see a World in a grain of Sand
> And a Heaven in a wild Flower
> Hold Infinity in the palm of your hand
> And Eternity in an Hour
>
> (*Auguries of Innocence*)

For Wordsworth, the creative imagination offers an insight into the nature of reality, making the poet a 'living soul' who can 'see into the life of things' (*Tintern Abbey*). It transforms objects, sees the hidden, often momentous, significance of even the meanest flower, the humblest creature or the child (the 'mighty prophet, seer blest' of Wordsworth's *Immortality*

Ode). And for Shelley, poetry, through the power of the poetic imagination, lifts the veil 'from the hidden beauty of the world, and makes familiar objects be as if they were not familiar' (*Defency of Poetry*).

It would be misleading to suggest that the English Romantic movement marked a complete break with the eighteenth century in poetry. In many ways, the poetry of Wordsworth, whose *Preface* of 1800 is the great Romantic manifesto, owes a profound debt to that of his predecessors; his roots, as F. R. Leavis pointed out in *Revaluation,* were deep in the eighteenth century. This may be illustrated by reference to many of his greater poems (see the separate article on Poetic Diction and Poetic. Language). Consider the following from a lesser-known poem:

> I was thy neighbour once, thou rugged Pile!
> Four Summer weeks I dwelt in sight of thee:
> I saw thee every day, and all the while
> Thy form was sleeping on a glassy sea.
>
> But welcome fortitude and patient cheer
> And frequent sights of what is to be borne!
> Such sights, or worse, as are before me here –
> Not without hope we suffer and we mourn.

In some respects, this poem is barely distinguishable from many an eighteenth-century one. The poetry is that of statement; it deals in abstractions ('fortitude', 'patient cheer'), and in the kind of poetic diction ('rugged pile', 'glassy sea') one thinks of as characteristic of Augustan poetry.

All the great Romantic poets attempt to give a mythic interpretation of the world. A myth is one story in a larger group called a mythology. Mythologies are evolved by cultural groups as attempts to explain the great mysteries of creation: how things began, the present condition of mankind, his aspirations and tendencies, the events outside his control to which he is subject, all with reference to the activities and attitudes of supernatural beings who preside over the destiny of things. A famous example is the biblical myth of the Tree of Knowledge, which attempts to account for the facts of the human situation, to answer such questions as these: Why should man, the crowning glory of creation, have to labour in order to live, and woman bring forth children in sorrow? This myth has affinities with certain Greek ones, such as those of Prometheus and Tiresias, in which the gods, jealous of man's knowledge, took their revenge by inflicting suffering upon him. One of the recurring themes of ancient myth is that of the longing of man for rebirth from which he could emerge renewed. This longing found confirmation in the primitive belief that the sun was a god who returned each night into the womb of his mother the sea, only to be reborn on the following day. Milton makes use of this myth at the end of *Lycidas*. The theme of rebirth is a universal one; it is found in the rites of springtime celebrated everywhere, in the myth of the phoenix, and is at the heart of all the great religions.

The English Romantic poets felt the necessity of finding a myth to express the state of man in the modern world. Shelley and Keats, seeing in classical myths a convincing version of the universal and timeless experience of mankind, set about giving them a new vitality. Blake, the most adventurous of poets, tried to create a whole new mythology, which he embodied in stories about great symbolic figures, on the ground, as he put it in *Jerusalem*, that 'I must create a system, or be enslaved by another man's.' Shelley aspired to create a new myth of the redemption of the earth, finding in Prometheus a saviour-figure and an appropriate hero for his political myth. In *Ode to the West Wind* he makes fruitful use of the myth of death and rebirth. Wordsworth who, like Byron, set out to create a mythology out of his own life, embodies mythic elements in his *Ode on the Intimations of Immortality*. The Platonic myth of heavenly pre-existence is the source of the poem, and, to mention only one detail, the venerable myth of the ocean as the ultimate source of life is behind the lines about 'the immortal sea / which brought us hither'. Coleridge, whose *Ancient Mariner* may be read as a version of the myth of rebirth, explains why he and his contemporaries found it so difficult to abandon classical myth:

> The intelligible forms of ancient poets,
> The fair humanities of old religion,
> The Power, the Beauty and the Majesty,
> That had their haunts in dale or piny mountain,
> Or forest by slow stream, or pebbly spring,

Or chasms and watery depths; all these have vanished.
They live no longer in the faith of reason!
But still the heart doth need a language, still
Doth the old instinct bring back the old names . . .

It is appropriate to contrast the Romantic emphasis on imagination and 'sensibility' with the neo-classic devotion to reason and good sense, and to stress the Romantic exaltation of the individual and of individual liberty, the rejection of restrictive rules and conventions. Other manifestations of English Romanticism were a revival of interest in the medieval past, with its associations of enchantment, mystery and wonder, the rediscovery and creative use of old ballads, a strong taste for the supernatural and the preternatural, for exotic narratives of adventure and discovery, an interest in the primitive and in wild nature, a sense of spiritual communion between the objects of external nature and the mind that perceives them.

Bibliography: L. P. Smith, *Words and Idioms*, 1925, Constable G. Tillotson, *On the Poetry of Pope,* 1938, Oxford University Press; Basil Willey, *The Eighteenth Century Background,* 1940, Chatto; W. J. Bate, *From Classic to Romantic,* Cambridge Mass., 1947, Harvard; A. O. Lovejoy, *Essays in the History of Ideas,* 1948, Johns Hopkins Press; John Butt, *The Augustan Age,* 1950, Hutchinson; J. W. H. Atkins, *English Literary Criticism, Seventeenth and Eighteenth Centuries,* 1951, Methuen; T. S. Eliot, *Selected Prose,* ed., John Hayward, 1953, Penguin; M. H. Abrams, *The Mirror and the Lamp,* 1953, Hutchinson; F. Kermode, *Romantic Image,* 1957, Routledge; D. Nichol Smith, *Some Observations on Eighteenth Century Poetry,* 1960, Oxford University Press; M. H. Abrams, ed., *The English Romantic Poets, Modern Essays in Criticism,* 1960, Oxford University Press; Maurice Bowra, *The Romantic Imagination,* 1961, Oxford University Press; R. Wellek, *Concepts of Criticism,* 1963, Yale University Press; A. Thorlby, *The Romantic Movement,* 1967, Longmans; N. Frye, *A Study of English Romanticism,* 1968, Random House; L. R. Furst, *Romanticism in Perspective,* 1969, Macmillan; D. Secretan, *Classicism,* 1973, Methuen; J. Sutherland, *A Preface to Eighteenth Century Poetry* 1975, Oxford University Press 1948/1963.

Paradox

The Oxford English Dictionary defines paradox as 'a statement seemingly self-contradictory or absurd, though possibly well-founded or essentially true'. This meaning, its accepted modern one, may be traced to the middle of the sixteenth century. Originally, however, paradoxes were views which contradicted accepted opinion. When Hamlet tells Ophelia that the idea that beauty leads virtuous people astray more readily than goodness can transform beauty into a good influence 'was sometime a paradox, but now the time gives it proof' (III, i, 115), he is using the word in its older sense.

There are two basic ways of regarding paradoxes – as verbal exercises (sometimes clever, sometimes trivial, sometimes embodiments of profound truths) or as major structural features of entire literary works. Examples of local paradox are Hamlet's 'I must be cruel only to be kind' (III, iv, 178); Milton's description of God: 'Dark with excessive bright thy skirts appear' (III, 380). and numerous lines from Shakespeare's sonnets ('With what I most enjoy contented least'; 'Consumed with that which it was nourished by').

As J. B. Leishman pointed out, the first considerable English poet to exploit the possibilities of paradox was John Donne. Many of Donne's poems are either extended paradoxes, founded on paradoxical ideas, or formed from whole strings of paradoxes. The theme of *The Will*, for example, is the paradoxical leaving of things to unsuitable recipients: gifts are bequeathed to those who already have too much of them, who will be insulted by them and despise them, and so forth:

> Before I sigh my last gasp, let me breathe,
> Great Love, some legacies; here I bequeath
> Mine eyes to Argus, if mine eyes can see,
> If they be blind, then Love, I give them thee;
> My tongue to fame; to ambassadors mine ears;
> To women or the sea, my tears.
> Thou, Love hast taught me heretofore
> By making me serve her who had twenty more,
> That I should give to none, but such, as had too much before.

In *The Anagram,* he argues that it is better to marry an old ugly
woman than a young and beautiful one, because the face of
the former can never change for the worse. *The Canonization* is
founded on the paradoxical notion that lovers are saints, and
offers to prove this by means of a series of paradoxes. In most
of Donne's poems, the most memorable assertions are liable
to be framed as paradoxes, often depending for their
effect on clever word-play:

> There should I see a sun, by rising set,
> And by that setting endless day beget;
> But that Christ on this Cross, did rise and fall,
> Sin had eternally benighted all . . .
>   (*Good Friday, 1613, Riding Westward*)

The most celebrated example of paradoxical structure in
Donne is the following:

> Death be not proud, though some have called thee
> Mighty and dreadful, for, thou art not so,
> For, those, whom thou think'st thou dost overthrow,
> Die not, poor death, nor yet canst thou kill me;
> From rest and sleep, which but thy pictures be,
> Much pleasure, then from thee, much more must flow,
> And soonest our best men with thee do go,
> Rest of their bones, and soul's delivery.
> Thou art slave to fate, chance, kings and desperate men,
> And dost with poison, war, and sickness dwell,
> And poppy, or charms can make us sleep as well,
> And better than thy stroke; why swell'st thou then?
> One short sleep past, we wake eternally,
> And death shall be no more, Death thou shalt die.

The arguments proposed in favour of the paradoxical proposi-
tion that death is ultimately harmless are themselves outrageously paradoxical. Sleep is an imitation of death and is
pleasant; therefore death, the real thing, must be even more
pleasant. Death is brought about by many disreputable
agents and associated with revolting processes, such as
poison, war and sickness. And finally, to clinch the argument,
the doctrine of immortality is invoked to show that death itself
faces ultimate annihilation.

The use of paradox as a basic structural device is a characteristic feature of the work of all the poets in the Donne tradition. Marvell's witty use of paradox in his major poetry is particularly satisfying. The central idea of *The Garden* is well described by J. B. Leishman: 'The paradox which Marvell, with such an exquisite mingling of seriousness and light-heartedness, is here maintaining is the great, the eternal, paradox of which Aristotle was aware when he recognized that the life of pure contemplation, though often incompatible with the exercise of those faculties and the performance of those duties which are necessary for the preservation of human society, was nevertheless the most divine kind of life and that, in spite of those who tell us to be content to think mortal thoughts and to leave immortal thoughts to the gods, we should strive so far as possible to make ourselves immortal by living in and through the exercise of that intellect which is the most potent element within us'. (*The Art of Marvell's Poetry*, 1968 edn., p. 308).

The seventeenth-century use of paradox is not confined to the Metaphysical poets. The doubts and affirmations in Milton's *Lycidas* take the form of paradoxes; the whole poem turns on a triumphant resolution of the great central paradox enunciated in the lines 'For Lycidas is dead, dead ere his prime' (line 8) and 'Weep no more, woful shepherds, weep no more / For Lycidas your sorrow is not dead' (lines 165–6). In *Paradise Lost,* as most commentators insist, Milton is much concerned with the implications of the paradox which lies at the heart of the Christian story, the paradox of the *felix culpa* or fortunate fall. In Book XII we have Adam's enunciation of the mysterious paradox towards which the entire poem has been tending from the beginning:

> O goodness infinite, goodness immense!
> That all this good of evil should produce,
> And evil turn to good. . . (469–71).

This outcome of Satan's activities has been anticipated very early in the poem:

> How all his malice served but to bring forth
> Infinite goodness, grace and mercy shown
> On man by him seduced. . . (I, 215–7)

And *Paradise Lost* has a paradoxical conclusion, Adam being left triumphant in the depth of his misery, Satan miserable at the height of his triumph, his scheme to undermine God's glory having the paradoxical effect of enhancing it.

In all his greater plays Shakespeare exploits the possibilities of verbal and structural paradox, the insistent preoccupation with it in *King Lear* being particularly remarkable., The memorable utterances of the play find their inevitable expression in paradoxes. When the Old Man says 'You cannot see your way' (IV, i, 17), Gloucester answers

> I have no way and therefore want no eyes;
> I stumbled when I saw.   (IV, i, 18–19).

The sight imagery of the play converges on the paradox that the blind may see better than the keen-sighted, since they are not misled by their eyes. Again, the splendidly dressed fare worse than the naked wretches pitied by Lear who, a failure at the height of his prosperity, achieves salvation in wretchedness and deprivation. The paradox of Lear's wisdom is that it is achieved in madness. 'The Lear' as R. B. Heilman points out, 'who introduced rationalistic procedures soon becomes irrational. Yet in his very irrationality he is capable of an insight which he did not have when he was apparently in full command of his faculties. This pattern is the burden of the madness pattern, which is the structural core of the play' (*This Great Stage*, Louisiana State University Press, p. 171). A further, and related, paradox is that the Fool exposes the folly of the officially wise Lear; as the latter falls to folly the Fool rises to wisdom.

Paradox is so intrinsic to human nature and life that poetry rich in paradox is valued as the reflection of central truths of human experience. Pope's consideration of mankind finds its inevitable expression in a series of paradoxes:

> A being darkly wise, and rudely great:
> With too much knowledge for the Sceptic side,
> With too much weakness for the Stoic's pride,
> He hangs between; in doubt to act, or rest,
> In doubt to deem himself a God, or Beast,
> In doubt his Mind or Body to prefer,
> Born but to die, and reasoning but to err. . . .

Created half to rise, and half to fall;
Great lord of all things, yet a prey to all;
Sole judge of Truth, in endless Error hurl'd:
The glory, jest, and riddle of the world!

It is reasonable to suggest that paradox may be identified in much of the poetry we find most satisfying, but some critics go further, and argue that the language of poetry is the language of paradox. Cleanth Books, for example, claims that 'there is a sense in which paradox is the language appropriate and inevitable to poetry. . . . It is the scientist whose truth requires a language purged of every trace of paradox; apparently the truth which the poet utters can be approached only in terms of paradox' (*The Well Wrought Urn*, 1947, p. 1). Traditionally, paradox was primarily intellectual, being most often associated with irony and satire. Brooks extends the application of the term beyond this, discovering a new range of paradox in what he calls 'the Romantic pre-occupation with wonder – the surprise, the revelation which puts the tarnished world in a new light'. A prime example is Wordsworth's attempt 'to show his audience that the common was really uncommon, the prosaic really poetic'. Whatever may be thought of this enlargement of the meaning of paradox, the argument that the language of poetry is the language of paradox is open to serious objection on philosophical grounds. Paradox and ambiguity, as J. M. Cameron points out, 'could only be the essentially distinguishing marks of poetry if we did not have a use for paradox and ambiguity in other forms of discourse. This is plainly false. . . . Even if we did establish instinctively that paradox and ambiguity are much commoner in poetic than in other forms of discourse, this would not affect my conclusion. For we could easily imagine a society where the opposite was true, where the poetry was comparatively limpid and other forms of discourse were crackling with paradox and knotty with ambiguity' (*The Night Battle*, 1962, 134–5).

Bibliography: A. O. Lovejoy, 'Milton and the Paradox of the Fortunate Fall', *Journal of English Literary History*, IV, 1937; Cleanth Brooks, *The Well Wrought Urn*, 1947, Methuen; R. B. Heilman, *This Great Stage: Image and Structure in King Lear*, 1948, Louisiana State University Press; J. B. Leishman, *The Monarch of Wit*, 1951, Hutchinson; *The Art of Marvell's Poetry*, 1966, Hutchinson.

Pastoral

A simple definition of pastoral is that it is a work in which the life of shepherds is portrayed, often in a conventional manner, the term also being extended to works dealing with country life generally. Pastoral is among the oldest and most universal of literary forms. In the third century B.C. the Greek poet Theocritus was writing pastoral poems describing the lives of Sicilian shepherds. His pastorals, and those of Virgil who imitated them, became models for all subsequent writers in the form.

It does not really do justice to pastoral poetry to describe it simply as dealing conventionally with the activities of shepherds or with the beauties of rural life. Very many pastoral poems, for example, present pastoral life in terms of a lost golden age; many others incorporate satire on contemporary abuses, while Christian writers, mindful of the large pastoral element in the Bible, of the biblical presentation of human life before the Fall as a golden age, found Christian pastoral a congenial form. A charming, fanciful account of the antiquity of pastoral poetry is provided by Pope in a preface to his own pastoral poems: 'As the keeping of flocks seems to have been the first employment of mankind, the most ancient sort of poetry was probably pastoral. 'Tis natural to imagine, that the leisure of those ancient shepherds admitting and inviting some diversion, none was so proper to that solitary and sedentary life as singing; and that in their songs they took occasion to celebrate their own felicity. From hence a Poem was invented, and afterwards improved to a perfect image of that happy time; which by giving us an esteem for the virtues of a former age, might recommend them to the present. And since the life of shepherds was attended with more tranquillity than any other rural employment, the Poets chose to introduce their Persons, from whom it received the name of Pastoral' ('A Discourse on Pastoral Poetry', *The Poems of Alexander Pope*, Twickenham edn.. 1968, p. 119).

One of the major developments in the history of pastoral
poetry was the tendency of its creators to associate the simple,
natural rustic life they celebrated with the almost universal
myth of a lost golden age. The association is well described by
Johan Huizinga: 'No other single illusion has charmed
humanity for so long and with such an ever fresh splendour as
the illusion of the pining shepherd's pipe and surprised
nymphs in rustling woods and murmuring brooks. The concept is very closely akin to that of the golden age, and constantly overlaps it; it is the golden age brought to life' (*Men
and Ideas*, 1966, p. 84). The myth of the golden age is found in
various versions in the work of all the great classical writers
and their modern imitators. It describes a time in the history
of the world when men lived in a state of perfect happiness, innocent of evil tendencies and free from cares and troubles.
One of the best-known versions of the myth is found in Ovid's
Metamorphoses: 'In the beginning was the Golden Age, when
men of their own accord, without threat of punishment,
without laws, maintained good faith and did what was right.
There were no penalties to be afraid of, no bronze tablets were
erected, carrying threats of legal action, no crowd of wrong-
doers, anxious for mercy, trembled before the face of their
judge: indeed there were no judges, men lived securely
without them. . . . The peoples of the world, untroubled by
any fears, enjoyed a leisurely and peaceful existence, and had
no use for soldiers. The earth itself, without compulsion, un-
touched by hoe, unfurrowed by any share, produced all things
spontaneously, and men were content with foods that grew
without cultivation'. (*The Metamorphoses of Ovid,* Translated by
Mary M. Innes, 1955, pp. 31–2).

Sophisticated poets, often living far from the scenes of rural
life they idealized in their work (Theocritus wrote his
pastorals in the court of King Ptolemy), tended to translate
their nostalgia for the simple values of pastoral existence into
a general lament for lost innocence and simplicity, with the
implication that things must once have been different. The
biblical story of the fall of Adam and Eve and of their idyllic
life in Eden has a central place in the literature of the golden
age. Milton's celebration of the theme of Eden as the golden
world is one of the glories of English pastoral poetry:

> Thus was this place,
> A happy rural seat of various view;
> Groves whose rich trees wept odorous gums and balm,
> Others whose fruit burnished with golden rind
> Hung amiable, Hesperian fables true. . . .
>
> (*Paradise Lost*, Book IV, 246 ff.)

The history of English pastoral poetry is almost a roll-call of all the great names. During the last quarter of the sixteenth century, lyrical and dramatic poetry tended to present idealized and idyllic pictures of the shepherd's life as a means of escape from the growning complexities of everyday life. Sir Philip Sidney's prose-work *Arcadia,* named after the idyllic world of leisure evoked by Virgil as the setting for his pastorals and which has since always stood for the ideal world of pastoral romance, and Edmund Spenser's *Shepheardes Calendar* are the best-known pastoral works of the age. Sidney's landscape has all the usual pastoral features: 'There were hills which garnished their proud heights with stately trees; humble valleys whose base estate seemed comforted with refreshing of silver rivers . . . . here a shepherd's boy piping, as though he should never be old; there a young shepherdess knitting, and withal singing, and it seemed that her voice comforted her hands to work. . .' This picture anticipates part of the 'cold Pastoral' scene on Keats's Grecian urn with its 'happy melodist . . . forever piping songs forever new' and its happy love 'forever panting and forever young'. A convincing case has been made for describing at least four of Shakespeare's plays (*The Two Gentlemen of Verona, Love's Labours Lost, A Midsummer Night's Dream,* and *As You Like It*) as pastoral comedies. In *As You Like It,* the Forest of Arden becomes in one of its aspects a typically pastoral haven where man can find relief from the conflicts and burdens of everyday life, and 'fleet the time carelessly, as they did in the golden world' (I, i, 109). Other Shakespearian plays with strong pastoral preoccupations are *The Winter's Tale* and *The Tempest.*

In seventeenth-century poetry, pastoral finds its most memorable expression in the work of Milton up to *Lycidas,* the greatest of the English pastoral elegies (Shelley's *Adonais,* Tennyson's *In Memoriam* and Arnold's *Thyrsis* are other examples of this form); in parts of *Paradise Lost,* and in Marvell's *Garden* poems. In *Lycidas,* we find (in the St. Peter passage) the fusion of pastoral with satire. This, as Peter Bayley has remarked, is not as surprising as it seems: 'Although pastoral and satire seem to be poles apart, the impulse behind both is the same. The satirist attacks the vices, follies and abuses of his day. However violent his onslaught may be, however savage his indignation, his motivation comes from an ambition for the good. So does that of the pastoralist. The satirist attacks his age for its imperfections and corruptions; the pastoralist celebrates the perfection of an age long past, an imagined age of simplicity and piety, of simple pleasure and contentment. It is a short step from nostalgic love of the past to bitter rejection of the present. While the classical pastoralists indulged in nostalgia but only by implication condemned their own time, the Renaissance pastoralist concerned himself much more roughly and openly to express his hatred of his own times. For a time pastoral became the form in which one wrote satire. The shepherd's cloak and classical name, and the implied remoteness of the time described gave useful concealment to the satirical aim of the writer, who could disclaim any specific, libellous or politically dangerous intention' (*Edmund Spenser: Prince of Poets,* 1971, p. 23).

The decline of traditional pastoral became quite pronounced in the eighteenth century. It is often suggested that the last major landmark was Pope's *Pastorals* (1709). However, the eighteenth century did see the appearance of a large body of poetry owing a debt to the pastoral tradition. In such poems as Goldsmith's *Deserted Village,* for example, we find praise for the idea of retirement from the busy world to the peace of the village, nostalgic memories of the innocent pleasures or rural life, the evocation of the lost innocence and joy of a happier age, contrasted altogether favourably with the unlovely present. But representative critics such as Samuel Johnson found pastoral unacceptable as a vehicle for serious ideas, as his attack on the use by Milton of pastoral conventions in *Lycidas* shows. Discontent with pastoral found a variety of outlets. Poets like John Gay and Jonathan Swift resorted to parody. In the most celebrated anti-pastoral poem of the century, *The Village* (1783), George Crabbe dismissed

the decorative conventions of classical pastoral as inadequate
to the expression of the grim realities of actual shepherd life:

> I grant indeed that fields and flocks have charms
> For him that grazes or for him that farms;
> But when amid such pleasing scenes I trace
> The poor laborious natives of the place,
> And see the midday sun, with fervid ray,
> On their bare heads and dewy temples play;
> While some, with feebler heads and fainter hearts,
> Deplore their fortune, yet sustain their parts,
> Then shall I dare these real ills to hide
> In tinsel trappings of poetic pride?
>
> (Book I, 39–48).

While disillusionment with the artificial conventions and
escapism of traditional pastoral was often expressed in the
eighteenth and nineteenth centuries, the tradition continued
to influence many poets, however much they modified it. The
work of Blake, Keats and Shelley is full of echoes of English
classical pastoral. The title of Wordsworth's *Michael: A
Pastoral Poem* (1800) shows how at the turn of the century the
term had taken on a new meaning, since Wordsworth is
writing not of the idealized life of remote beings in a golden
age, but of the harsh, even tragic, lot of contemporary
countrymen. In *The Prelude,* Wordsworth points out that the
shepherds of his poems are not those belonging to 'A bright
tradition of the golden age', but the actual modern shepherds
whose ways were 'the unluxuriant products of a life / Intent
on little but substantial needs' (Book VIII, 208–9). The
nineteenth-century poet Thomas Hood expressed a common
point of view when he wrote: 'The Golden Age is not to be
regilt / Pastoral is gone out and Pan extinct'. But pastoral was
not really 'gone out', as some of Matthew Arnold's best-
known poems (among them *The Scholar Gipsy* and *Thyrsis*)
testify. Although in 1899 Yeats could write that 'The woods of
Arcady are dead / And over is their antique joy', the pastoral
mood was to dominate much of the English poetry of the first
two decades of the twentieth century. The 'Georgian' poets, to
quote one of their critics, 'specialized in country sentiment

and the pursuit of Beauty'. Of Edmund Blunden, one of the most distinguished of these poets, F. R. Leavis wrote: 'Mr Blunden's retreat is to an Arcadia that is rural England seen, not only through memories of childhood, but through poetry and art. Eighteenth-century meditative pastoral is especially congenial to him; he takes over even the nymphs and their attendant classicalities.' (*New Bearings in English Poetry*, 1950 edn., p. 67). And although the mid twentieth-century sensibility might be considered inimical to pastoral, it flourished in the poetry of Dylan Thomas, whose *Fern Hill*, for example, has many of the traditional trappings: golden, magical landscapes, nostalgia for the lost happiness of earlier days (in this case innocent, carefree childhood), the sad consciousness of change, as 'the children green and golden' follow time 'out of grace'.

In the hands of some recent critics, pastoral has lost much of its earlier meaning and acquired a more extensive field of reference. 'If pastoral lives for us at all at the present time', writes Peter Marinelli, 'it lives by a capacity to move out of its old haunts in the Arcadian pastures and to inhabit the ordinary country landscapes of the modern world, daily contracted by the encroachment of civilization and as a consequence daily more precious as a projection of our desires for simplicity. In the modern sense, pastoral is a very broad and very general term far removed from the more specific and distinct meaning attributed to it in earlier times. It scarcely has reference to a literature about actual shepherds, much less about Arcadians. For us it has come to mean any literature which deals with the complexities of human life against a background of simplicity. All that is necessary is that memory and imagination should conspire to render a not too distant past of comparative innocence as more pleasurable than a harsh present, overwhelmed either by the growth of technology or the shadows of advancing age' (*Pastoral*, 1971, p. 3). In the modern understanding of pastoral, the idealized simplicities of shepherd life give way to those of childhood (as often in de la Mare, Dylan Thomas and Patrick Kavanagh, for example). One of the best-known champions of the new application of the term, William Empson, extends it to include works as varied as *Alice in Wonderland* and the proletarian novel (the simple working man at the mercy of a complicated society). Those who seek to give pastoral a 'modern' connotation are never short of examples. A recent critic has proposed golf as a characteristically modern pastoral preoccupation: 'A modern golf course is a miniature Arcadia, a land of green grass and gentle streams; a land, moreover, where one plays rather than works. The fanatical devotion to the game of golf, from presidents to paupers, testifies to how much these green plots are cherished. And although nothing else – great buildings, venerable monuments, nature itself – seems proof against real estate developers, road builders and other eroders of modern life, the golf course often seems miraculously inviolate against the inroads of urban blight' (Thomas McFarland, *Shakespeare's Pastoral Comedy*, North Carolina, 1972, p. 42).

Bibliography: W. W. Greg, *Pastoral Poetry and Pastoral Drama,* 1906; W. Empson, *Some Versions of Pastoral,* 1950, Chatto; J. E. Congleton, *Theories of Pastoral Poetry in England,* 1684–1798, Florida 1952; Hallett Smith, *Elizabethan Poetry,* Cambridge Mass, 1952; F. Kermode, ed., *English Pastoral Poetry from the Beginnings to Marvell,* 1952; Eleanor T. Lincoln, *Pastoral and Romance, Modern Essays in Criticism,* 1969; P. Marinelli, Pastoral, 1971, Methuen; T. McFarland, *Shakespeare's Pastoral Comedy,* Chapel Hill, North Carolina, 1972; J. Barrell and J. Bull eds., *The Penguin Book of English Pastoral Verse,* 1974.

Pastoral Elegy

The English word elegy is derived from the Greek word for a lament. Strictly the term applies to any serious meditation on transience, human or otherwise. Gray's *Elegy in a Country Churchyard,* for example, deals with the passing of things as well as of men. But most of the important English elegies are formal laments on the deaths of particular men: Milton's *Lycidas* mourns Edward King; Shelley's *Adonais* laments the death of Keats, Tennyson's *In Memoriam* the death of Hallam; Arnold's *Thyrsis* the death of Clough. Many of the more important English elegies are pastoral in form.

The origins of the pastoral elegy lie in classical antiquity. The elaborate conventions employed by pastoral elegists are most conveniently illustrated by reference to Milton's *Lycidas,* by common consent the supreme English achievement in the form. The most basic convention is the representation of both the mourner (Milton's 'uncouth swain') and the subject of the elegy (Lycidas) as shepherds tending their flocks (lines 23–36). It is worthy of note that Milton, here writing a Christian pastoral elegy, makes effective use of the conventional association of pastor and pastoral with biblical themes: pastor is priest as well as shepherd; Christ is the Good Shepherd; the Christian faithful are a flock; the Church is a sheepfold, and so on. The elegist (best described as the lyric speaker because he is not necessarily to be identified at all points with the poet) begins his lament by invoking the muses of classical poetry and makes numerous references to other mythological personages (lines 15–22). Nature is invited to join the elegist in mourning the shepherd's death (lines 37–49), while the nymphs and his other appropriate guardians are accused of dereliction of duty (lines 50–63). There follows a procession of appropriate mourners (lines 88–111).

The elegist poses questions arising from the untimely death of his subject: questions about the justice of a providence that can let men like King die before their prime while sparing the unworthy and even the wicked. He also indulges in satirical invective against the corrupt state of the contemporary

118

Church (appropriate in this case because Lycidas is mourned as priest as well as poet). The fusion of satire with pastoral was common in Renaissance elegies (see the article on Pastoral). Another feature of *Lycidas,* not found in all pastoral elegies, but still quite common, is the floral passage (lines 133–151). Finally, there is the conventional optimistic close, the transformation of the earlier bleak statement of the shepherd's death ('For Lycidas is dead, dead ere his prime') to the unqualified assurance of 'For Lycidas your sorrow is not dead'. The Christian elegist recognises in death an apotheosis – a means of giving mortals entry to a higher and happier state (lines 165–185). Graham Hough comments well on this aspect of the poem: 'A consecrated feature of the traditional elegy is the turn at the close: after the lament, the recantation – he is not dead: but the cast which is given to this defiant assertion of immortality depends on the philosophy of the writer, pagan, Christian or modern pantheist. Milton, incurably classic as well as Christian, gives us two versions of the fate of Lycidas – he has become a nature-spirit, the genius of the shore; and he is received among the solemn troops and sweet societies of the saints in heaven' (*The Romantic Poets,* 1953, p. 147). With the Miltonic version of immortality (which leans heavily on St. John), compare that envisaged by Shelley in his lament for Keats: 'He is made one with Nature; there is heard / His voice in all her music, from the moan / Of thunder, to the song of night's sweet bird' (*Adonais,* XLII).

Milton's narrative technique in *Lycidas* calls for comment. It is important to recognize that he is at pains to identify the main speaker of the poem with someone other than himself. This becomes especially obvious when one has read the poem through and reached the last eight lines beginning: 'Thus sang the uncouth swain . . . ' The point of these lines is that they draw attention to the fact that all that has gone before has either been spoken or narrated by 'the uncouth swain' (the unknown or rustic poet) who is not to be confused with Milton himself speaking in his own voice or person. In thus employing the device of an unnamed rustic signer or speaker, Milton is making use of a persona or character or mask. This rustic speaker refers to the current state of affairs in England, describes the appearance and quotes the statements of other speakers, including Camus, Phoebus and St. Peter. He also expresses his own thoughts and changing moods, and conveys, by implication, something of his own character. Because of this, *Lycidas* is a dramatic lyric as well as a pastoral elegy, with a setting, an occasion, a chief character and several subordinate characters. These last characters may be taken as expressing the speaker's own views: St. Peter, for example, is made to express ideas on the corrupt state of the Church of England which the speaker presumably shares. It is worth noting that it is only in the closing eight lines that Milton takes over as omniscient narrator, in his own person and voice, and that to mark this transition he changes the versestructure of his poem; the last eight lines are a stanza and therefore technically distinct from the rest of the poem. This concluding stanza puts the entire poem in a dramatic framework.

The aspect of *Lycidas* most commonly discussed is the presence or absence of real emotion; the engagement or otherwise of the poet's feelings, the 'sincerity' of the poem. The following comments illustrate the range of critical response to the question, posed in its most memorable form by Samuel Johnson in his *Life of Milton*.

(a) Most readers agree that Milton was not deeply grieved at King's death, as they agree that the poem is great. If it is great, it must contain deep feeling of some sort. What then is this deep feeling all about? Most criticism of *Lycidas* is off the mark, because it fails to distinguish between the nominal and the real subject, what the poem professes to be about and what it is about. It assumes that Edward King is the real, whereas he is but the nominal subject. Fundamentally *Lycidas* concerns Milton himself; King is but the excuse for one of Milton's most personal poems. This cannot be proved: it can only be deduced from the impression the poem leaves.

(E. M. W. Tillyard. *Milton*, 1930, p. 80)

(b) The elegy is not, as often thought, merely a lament for an individual, but an elaborate literary memorial intended to perpetuate his memory. The duty or practical job of the elegist, as of the sculptor in similar circumstances, is to commemorate the dead by creating a worthy and en-

during work of art; only if the work endures as literature
has the intention of the elegy been fulfilled. Consequently
the predominant motive of the elegist, however sincere his
personal grief, must be an artistic one, implying a literary
detachment such as is evident in the opening and closing
lines of *Lycidas*. Milton chose to work in a form of the
elegy sanctioned by long tradition and by the outstanding
names of Theocritus, Virgil and Spenser; and the poem is
partly inspired, as all Milton's greatest work is, by a
literary ambition – the ambition to produce in English a
consummate example of the pastoral elegy. His success in
this literary ambition measures his success as an elegist;
but for *Lycidas* the name of Edward King would long ago
have been forgotten.

(B. A. Wright, *John Milton, Shorter Poems*, 1938, p. 173)

(c) It has been pointed out that Milton did not necessarily
have any close friendship with King and that he therefore
took the young man's death as a convenient peg on which
to hang his elegy. The expression of grief is thus, we are
inclined to say, conventional, and the elegy itself a conventional poem. But the term should not imply that
Milton's feelings are not seriously engaged: the question is
rather, what is the real subject? What theme does engage
the poet's feelings? The answer can be found in the poem
itself: Milton is at his most conventional in describing his
personal association with King . . . . and he can afford to
be conventional here, for what counts in the poem is not
Edward King as an individual but rather what King
stands for, the young poet and pastor. But is Milton is not
deeply concerned with King as a person, he is deeply concerned, and as a young poet personally involved, with a
theme – which is that of the place and meaning of poetry
in a world which seems at many points inimical to it . . . It
is this theme that dominates the poem.

(Cleanth Brooks and John Edward Hardy,
Poems of Mr. John Milton, New York, 1951, p. 172)

(d) The risk with biographical readings is that they will ignore artistic aptness. If we foist into the poem Milton the
man, then St. Peter's lines on the bad priests will seem a

'digression', the expression of Milton's personal feelings rather than the creation of a poetic relevance. It is true that in this case Milton himself must bear some of the blame – not for any words which he wrote in the poem, but for some words which he subsequently wrote above it. When it was first published in the volume of obsequies for Edward King in 1638, *Lycidas* had needed no headnote. Reprinting it in 1645, Milton explained its provenance: 'In this Monody the Author bewails a learned friend, unfortunately drown'd in his Passage from Chester on the Irish Seas, 1637'. A pity that Milton did not leave it at that. Between 1638 and 1645, Archbishop Laud had fallen from favour, and Milton could not resist giving himself a pat on the back: 'And by occasion fortells the ruine of our corrupted Clergy then in their height'. But though Milton's indictment of the bad priests is certainly relevant to Laud, it is not limited to any such instance. As readers our first duty is to the poem Milton wrote in 1637, not to the headnote which he added eight years later. Despite his grim glee in 1645, Milton had not included the attack on bad priests merely in order to give vent to his personal feelings, but because of its artistic relevance.

(Christopher Ricks, ed., *English Poetry and Prose,*
1540–1674, pp. 260–261)

Bibliography: T. P. Harrison and H. J. Leon, eds., *The Pastoral Elegy: An Anthology,* 1939, Austin, Texas; C. A. Partrides, *Lycidas: The Tradition and the Poem,* 1961, Holt, Rinehart and Winston; J. B. Leishman, *Milton's Minor Poems,* 1969, Hutchinson; A. F. Potts, *The Elegiac Mode,* 1967.

Poetic Diction and Poetic Language

Language is best defined as the whole body of words and the methods of combining them (word-order and so forth). Diction signifies the actual vocabulary used by a writer. The terms 'poetic diction' and 'poetic language' are often carelessly employed as if they stood for the same thing, whereas diction is really only an element of language.

In the mid-eighteenth century, the poet Thomas Gray declared that 'the language of the age is never the language of poetry', by which he meant that poets have traditionally used language which differs significantly from that of everyday conversation or even from that of educated prose. Gray's claim needs to be qualified: the language of Shakespeare and of the seventeenth-century Metaphysicals, for example, is often close to that of current educated speech. Coleridge had this in mind when he drew the following contrast between seventeenth century poets and his own contemporaries: 'One great distinction I appeared to myself to see plainly, between even the characteristic faults of our elder poets and the false beauties of the moderns. In the former, from Donne to Cowley, we find the most fantastic out-of-the-way thoughts, but in the most pure and genuine mother English; in the latter, the most obvious thoughts, in language the most fantastic and arbitrary' (*Biographia Literaria*). However, very many English poets up to our own time would have accepted the notion of a specifically 'poetic language', varying from age to age, but differing essentially in such respects as diction, syntax and rhythm from that of any kind of prose.

Nowadays, when critics use such terms as poetic language and poetic diction, they are most often thinking of Milton and the eighteenth-century neo-classic poets. In the eighteenth century, in particular, there was widespread agreement among critics and poets that a distinction must be preserved between 'poetical' and 'non-poetical' subjects; not all topics were deemed worthy of serious poetical treatment, with the result that the diction of 'serious' poetry was restricted. The dominant impression made by eighteenth-century poetry on one modern critic is that 'words are thrusting at the poem and being fended off from it; however many poems these poets wrote, certain words would never be allowed into the poem, except as a disastrous oversight'. Again, in the eighteenth century, the various poetic genres – epic, elegy, ode, formal satire – were seen as quite distinct from each other and as requiring different kinds of poetic language. The diction of Pope's satires and epistles, for example, differs little from that of good prose; when he is writing in some more 'exalted' form – the elegy or the ode – he uses a distinctly 'poetic' diction.

Various elements of poetic diction can be isolated. One of these, not very common in good poems but quite so in bad ones, is the use of stock adjective-noun combinations: 'the bright crocus and the blue violet', 'the fair fields', 'the radiant sky', 'the verdant meadow', 'the curling vines' and so forth. In his *Essay on Criticism,* Pope satirizes the endless use by bad poets of stereotyped phrases: 'Where'er you hear the cooling western breeze / In the next line it flutters through the trees'. Most modern popular songs make similar repetitious use of a narrow range of words and phrases. Another, even more striking, aspect of poetic diction is the use of periphrasis, which means calling common, everyday things by most uncommon names, generally in an attempt to make them dignified enough for mention in serious poetry. Periphrasis is found in the poetry of all ages. Milton uses it admirably in *Paradise Lost* ('precious bane' for gold is an example); Pope talks of the moon as 'the refulgent lamp of night', and of a sportsman shooting game as follows:

He lifts the Tube and levels with his eye
Straight a short Thunder breaks the Frozen Sky
(*Windsor Forest,* 129-20)

Tennyson refers to King Arthur's beard as 'the knightly growth that fringed his lips'.

Obviously, the success of periphrasis varies. Many readers of eighteenth-century poetry grow tired of reading repeated references to sheep as 'the fleecy flock' and to birds as 'the feathered tribe'. Sometimes the effect can be more unfor-

tunate, as when a spade is called 'the implement rectangular /
That turneth up the soil'. And sometimes, of course,
periphrasis is used with intentionally comic effect: in *The Rape
of the Lock,* Pope calls a scissors 'the glittering Forfex' and 'the
fatal Engine'. It is true that in the eighteenth century, particularly in the hands of inferior poets, poetic diction could be
used as a handy substitute for close, accurate observation and
description. In the worst examples, adjectives singled out
some fairly obvious attribute of the nouns they qualified, or
were vaguely decorative. The ocean is 'the watery deep' or
'the watery plain'; fish are 'the watery race' and so on. But
against this, one must set the practice of the best eighteenth-
century poets, who, as Geoffrey Tillotson points out, use
language, including poetic diction, with admirable
scrupulousness. He cites a passage from Thomson's *Winter:*

                          the foodless wilds
Pour forth their brown inhabitants. The hare
Though timorous of heart, and hard beset
By death in various forms, dark snares and dogs
And more unpitying man, the garden seeks,
Urg'd in by fearless want. The bleating kind
Eye the bleak heaven, and next the glistening earth
With looks of dumb despair; then, sad dispersed
Dig for the withered herb through heaps of snow.

Tillotson comments: "Here the diction is parcel of the meaning. 'Brown inhabitants' is a neat way of grouping creatures
which inhabit the scene described and whose brownness is the
most evident thing about them in the snow. 'Bleating kind' is
anything but an unthinking substitute for 'sheep'. Thomson is
saying: we think of sheep as creatures who bleat, but they are
silent enough in the snow; it is the dumb eye and not the voice
that tells us of their despair' (*Augustan Poetic Diction,* 19, p. 42).
And when Thomson writes of birds as 'feather'd youth', he is
not using a routine formula: he means that the birds he is
describing, though they are young, are not too young to have
feathers.

A further element in poetic diction is the use of learned,
archaic and Latinized words to create impressive effects, to

raise the style of a poem to accommodate it to an exalted subject. English poetry has a vast store of 'poetic' words and
phrases which can be studied in the work of poets of every
generation. When Milton writes of the 'gory visage' of
Orpheus or the 'oozy locks' of Lycidas he is using poetic diction; so is Keats when he calls his nightingale 'light-winged
Dryad of the trees', or his urn a 'sylvan historian', or when he
sees 'barred clouds bloom the soft-dying day' (*To Autumn*).
Milton's *Paradise Lost* is a mine of poetic diction and distinc-
tively 'poetic' language. In the epic, Milton Latinized much of
his diction and distorted the normal English word-order (in
the opening lines of Book One, the main verb does not appear
until the beginning of line six). Milton proceeds in this way in
order to achieve the magnificence and remoteness from everyday reality which he believed his epic subject demanded. It
must be said that there are times when it is difficult to be certain whether some apparently unusual word or phrase is really an example of poetic diction. Milton's 'optic glass' for
Galileo's telescope looks like poetic diction, but in Milton's
day this was a common enough term.

The notion of poetic diction and of a specifically poetic
language came under severe attack in Wordsworth's *Preface to
Lyrical Ballads* (1800). Here Wordsworth argued that there
was 'no essential difference between the language of prose and
metrical composition', and that poetry should be written in
'language really used by men'. He objected to the 'gaudy and
inane phraseology' of many eighteenth-century poems which
he found 'unnatural' and 'artificial'. The tone of the *Preface*
would lead one to expect to find in Wordsworth's own poetry
a complete break with eighteenth-century poetic language. In
fact, he often ignores his own critical standards by compiling
a poetic diction of his own which is strikingly reminiscent of
what his Preface rejects. The 'beauteous forms', 'sensations
sweet', 'corporeal frame', 'the deep and gloomy wood' of
Tintern Abbey would have appeared perfectly at home in any
eighteenth-century poem. Geoffrey Tillotson points out that
'the passionate attack on eighteenth-century poetic diction
made by Wordsworth and Coleridge, whom we think of as
nineteenth-century poets, is all the more passionate because
the eighteenth century is in their blood and will not be expelled' (*Augustan Poetic Diction*, p. 23).

The 'modern' movement in English poetry dating from the early decades of the twentieth century marked a significant break with tradition in the matter of poetic diction. Most modern English poets have little use for a special poetic vocabulary distinct from that of prose. The achieved aim of such modern masters as Yeats and Eliot has been to make use of a somewhat heightened version of the current language. The ideal is admirably expressed by T. S. Eliot in *Little Gidding:* 'The common word exact without vulgarity / The formal word precise but not pedantic'. Eighteenth and nineteenth-century poets restricted the diction of poetry by avoiding certain topics (and therefore a wide selection of words) as 'unpoetical'. But the dominant twentieth-century view of poetic language is also restrictive, for a totally different reason. While other generations of poets tended to avoid 'unpoetical', 'low' and 'commonplace' diction in serious poems, most modern ones tend to shun words with 'poetical' associations. If a modern poet avoided contemporary colloquial idiom and composed an elaborately beautiful poem in, say, the style of *Paradise Lost* or that of Tennyson's *Lotos Eaters,* made free use of such words as 'orb', 'fragrant', 'refulgent', 'wondrous', 'beauteous' and so on, he would not command very serious critical attention. These words and many like them are 'out', so, in a sense, the remaining permissible ones constitute a modern poetic diction. Words such as 'loaf', 'bun', 'dump' and 'pig' may not be thought of as particularly poetical, but they are much more likely to find a place in a modern poem than are the overworked elements of the traditional poetical vocabulary. Eliot uses 'low' and 'modern' words in a serious poem like *The Waste Land;* Tennyson confines his use of these to his comic pieces and dialect poems. It remains true that a few popular modern anthology pieces preserve eighteenth- and nineteenth-century traditions in poetic diction. The poems of Walter de la Mare are outstanding examples ('Is there anybody there? said the Traveller / Knocking the moonlit door / And his horse in the darkness champed the grasses / Of the forest's ferny floor'). But then de la Mare is commonly regarded as something of an oddity, and does not enjoy serious critical recognition.

The following is a representative range of comment on the subject of poetic language.

(a) My purpose was to imitate, and as far as possible to adopt, the very language of men . . . There will also be found in these volumes little of what is usually called poetic diction; as much pains has been taken to avoid it, as is usually taken to produce it; this has been done for the reason already alleged, to bring my language near to the language of men . . . A large portion of the language of every good poem can in no respect differ from that of good prose. We will go further. It may safely be affirmed, that there neither is, nor can be, any essential difference between the language of prose and metrical composition.

(Wordsworth, *Preface to Lyrical Ballads,* 1800)

(b) Wordsworth's standard was wrong to start with, for he was claiming that the 'language' of poetry could and should be the language of prose. It can never be that, if what is meant by language is that of which diction is a part. 'Language' in this total sense includes – to mention one constituent other than diction – rhythm; and poetry, because of its stricter rhythm, has a different language from prose, even though it uses the same words.

(Geoffrey Tilotson, *Augustan Poetic Diction,* 1964, p. 85)

(c) The highest poetry can be written in what is, literally speaking, the vocabulary of the most ordinary prose; but when it is – for instance, 'The rest is silence', or 'To-morrow and to-morrow and to-morrow', or 'Put out the light', there is always some *additional* meaning which, in ordinary prose, the words do not bear.

(George Saintsbury, *The Peace of the Augustans,* 1916, p. 10)

(d) It would be misleading to represent Milton's influence upon diction as entirely beneficial. The strongly Latinic, learned and grandiloquent vocabulary of his epic, though admirably adapted to Pandemonic councils and the rebellion of the archangels, was a dangerous model for mediocre bards who were dealing with prosaic themes. Unfortunately, also, the most influential of his early followers exaggerated his lofty and unusual Latinisms, or at least did not modify them when dealing with very different subject-matter. As a result, bombast and blank verse became almost synonymous.

(R. D. Havens, *The Influence of Milton on English Poetry*, 1922, p. 66)

(e) Milton reveals a very considerable indebtedness, not merely to the diction of Shakespeare, but to that of many other sixteenth- and seventeenth-century poets, some very minor ones. Some of his most memorable phrases are often appropriations; with certain additions and modifications of his own, of what were almost *clichés* . . . . Milton's 'industrious and select reading' embraced, one must assume, English as well as classical and Italian poets, and almost certainly demanded the companionship of a notebook into which he copied any passage or phrase, any 'elegances or flowers of speech', which happened to take his fancy and of which he felt that he might at some time be able to make good use himself . . . He sometimes complied with the contemporary academic taste for the ingenious comparison, but it would no more have occurred to him to cultivate in his English poetry that out-of-one's-own-head kind of originality which Carew praised in Donne than it would have occurred to him to try to write Latin poetry as though no one had ever written it before.

(L. B. Leishman, *Milton's Minor Poems*, 1969, p. 151)

(f) The effect of the return to ordinary language in the present century has been far-reaching. The feeling that there are intrinsically poetical and unpoetical sectors of the language has been repudiated. Much of the old paraphernalia of poetic expression (e.g. archaism) has been overthrown, and poets have eagerly delved into the most unlikely resources, such as the terminology of aeronautics and finance. Pound, Eliot and the poets of the 'thirties showed their determination to be rid of orthodox restrictions of choice by making use of flagrantly prosy and vulgar aspects of everyday usage. In the new poetry of the fifties, this flamboyance has given way to a more sober and easy acceptance of colloquialism, even slang, as a fit medium of poetic expression. A good example is Philip

Larkin's *Toads* . . . . Its idiomatic familiarity of tone is in many ways typical of recent British poetry.

On the other hand, poetic language cannot come too close to the 'ordinary' language of the day. If it does, it runs the danger of another kind of banality, an undistinguished style which is perhaps easier to illustrate from one of Wordsworth's well-known experiments, such as *Simon Lee, the Old Huntsman*, rather than from contemporary poetry. So we may think of the successful poet as avoiding the banality of two dimensions: the banality of the poetic convention of the past; and the banality of the everyday usage of the present. These two forces pull in opposite directions, and there is rarely a firm balance between them.

G. N. Leech, *A Linguistic Guide to English Poetry*, 1969, pp. 23–4)

See separate articles on Epic and Mock-Heroic, Neo-classic and Romantic, and Pastoral Elegy.

Bibliography: T. Quayle, *Poetic Diction, A Study of Eighteenth Century Verse*, 1924, Methuen; O. Barfield, *Poetic Diction*, 1928, Faber & Gwyer (later Faber & Faber); T. S. Eliot, *Selected Essays*, 1932, Faber; *Selected Prose*, 1953, Penguin; *On Poetry and Poets*, 1957, Faber; D. Davie, *Purity of Diction in English Verse*, 1952, Chatto & Windus; G. W. Tillotson, *Augustan Prose Diction*, 1961, Athlone Press; C. Ricks, *Milton's Grand Style* 1963, Oxford University Press; C. B. Cox and A. E. Dyson, *Modern Poetry: Studies in Practical Criticism*, 1969, E. Arnold; *The Practical Criticism of Poetry*, 1971, E. Arnold; I. A. Richards, *Practical Criticism*, 1928, Routledge and Keegan Paul; A. C. Partridge, *The Language of Modern Poetry*, 1976, Deutsch.

Rhythm and Metre

It is impossible to talk about metre in verse without at the same time referring to rhythm. As we read any passage, whether prose or verse, we are conscious of a rhythm, which is the pattern we find in the stress or emphasis we give to the words as we read them. In verse, this pattern is ordered into regular units of approximately the same size. The result is metre, which may be defined as the recurrence in a line of poetry of a regular rhythmic unit. English metres are generally described in terms of the relationship between the weak and strong stresses in a given line. Traditionally, prosodists have taken the foot to be the basic metrical unit (but see below). The foot is is a combination of stressed and unstressed syllables. The line of English verse (following classical convention) is named according to the number of feet it contains. It is obvious that the stressed and unstressed syllables in a given foot can occur in different combinations. When the foot consists of an unstressed followed by a stressed syllable, it is called *iambic*; when it consists of two unstressed syllables followed by a stressed one it is called *anapestic*; a stressed followed by an unstressed syllable makes a *trochaic* foot. It is also obvious that the number of feet in a line of verse can vary. A metrical line consisting of two feet is called *dimeter*; if it has three feet it is called *trimeter*; a four-foot line is called a *tetrameter*, and a line having five feet is called a *pentameter*. The metre of any line of verse is described by combining the conventional names for the kind of foot which predominates in it (iambic, anapestic, etc.) and for the number of feet it contains (tetrameter, pentameter, etc.). For example, the dominant metre of Shakespeare's sonnets is iambic pentameter, the norm being ten syllables, every second one of which is stressed.

The problem about reading a line or passage of poetry in such a way as to conform to the strict metrical pattern is that the result can often by a monotonous sing-song. In practice what frequently happens is that the rhythm of the reading voice resists the pattern imposed by the 'official' metrical norm. To test the validity of this, try reading the opening lines of Shakespeare's sonnets 30 and 60 as strict iambic pentameters. G. N. Leech points out that it has become widely accepted that 'versification is a question of the interplay between two planes of structure: the ideally regular, quasi-mathematical pattern called metre, and the actual rhythm the language insists on – sometimes called the prose rhythm' (*A Linguistic Guide to English Poetry*, 1969, p. 103). The same writer argues that what he calls the measure or unit of rhythm is a more reliable concept than the foot in English prosody. His distinction, and the value of his suggestion, can be assessed by looking at the way in which he scans a line of regular iambic pentameter. He separates measures by vertical lines, and feet by horizontal brackets:

The|ploughman|homeward|plods his|weary|way

A close study of its rhythms often helps to determine the value of a poem. It is obviously unsatisfactory when the poem moves mechanically when its theme is one requiring sensitive treatment, when the lines run along monotonously without variation of stress or emphasis, when movement bears no real relation to sense when it should faithfully reflect the patterns of thought and feeling behind the words. Good rhythm is flexible: it follows the varying contours of feeling and attitude which are part of genuine poetic expression of any kind. In a good poem, rhythm, feeling and ideas are inseparable; in many bad ones, rhythm is at odds with meaning or independent of it, remaining uniform, for example, despite changes in tone or meaning. Poets who have nothing personal to communicate often tend to lapse into easy, mechanical rhythms.

The best test of these matters is a sensitive reading aloud. In the case of Wordsworth's sonnet *Surprised by Joy*, for example, such a reading demands constant shifts of tone, emphasis, modulation and tempo:

> Surprised by joy – impatient as the Wind
> I turned to share the transport – O! with whom
> But Thee deep buried in the silent tomb,
> That spot which no vicissitude can find?

Love, faithful love, recalled thee to my mind –
 But how could I forget thee? Through what power,
 Even for the least division of an hour,
Have I been so beguiled as to be blind
To my most grievous loss? – That thought's return
 Was the worst pang that sorrow ever bore,
Save one, one only, when I stood forlorn,
 Knowing my heart's best treasure was no more;
That neither present time, nor years unborn
 Could to my sight that heavenly face restore.

Here a genuinely personal experience is being successfully conveyed. Intensity of feeling and emotional sincerity are enacted in complex rhythmical effects and delicate inflections. By contrast, the rhythms of another Wordsworth sonnet, *O Friend I know not*, are much less subtle:

 O Friend! I know not which way I must look
 For comfort, being, as I am, opprest,
 To think that now our life is only drest
 For show; mean handy-work of craftsman, cook
 Or groom! We must run glittering like a brook
 In the open sunshine, or we are unblest:
 The wealthiest man among us is the best:
 No grandeur now in nature or in book
 Delights us. Rapine, avarice, expense,
 This is idolatry; and these we adore:
 Plain living and high thinking are no more:
 The homely beauty of the good old cause
 Is gone; our peace, our fearful innocence,
 And pure religion breathing household laws.

The poem moves at a leisurely pace and demands a rather solemn, unvaried, relaxed reading. It is impressive at one level, but the lack of rhythmic variety reflects the comparative absence of complex feeling.

 To take a more extreme set of examples, one might contrast the urgent, vital rhythms of Donne's best dramatic lyrics with the smooth, relaxed, incantatory movement of Tennyson's *Lotos Eaters*. Donne, in such poems as *The Good-Morrow* and

The Sunne Rising is dramatising experiences; he must therefore
keep close to the rhythms of colloquial speech:

> Busy old fool, unruly sunne,
> Why dost thou thus,
> Through windows, and through curtains call on us?
> Must to thy motions lovers' seasons run?
> Saucy pedantique wretch, go chide
> Late school-boys, and sour prentices. . . . .
>
> (*The Sunne Rising*)

Tennyson is depicting the languorous charms of an idyllic
existence: his rhythms harmonize perfectly with the mood of
dreamy intoxication he is trying to convey:

> There is sweet music here that softer falls
> Than petals from blown roses on the grass,
> Or night-dews on still waters between walls
> Of shadowy granite, in a gleaming pass;
> Music that gentlier on the spirit lies,
> Than tired eyelids upon tired eyes. . . .

Donne's ryhthms would be inappropriate to Tennyson's subject as Tennyson's would be to Donne's. The rhythms of
Shakespeare's finest dramatic blank verse are necessarily
close to those of colloquial speech. Those of *Paradise Lost,* on
the other hand, are mainly quite remote from them. F. R.
Leavis complained that in *Paradise Lost* 'the stylised gesture
and movement has no particular work to do, but functions by
rote, of its own momentum, in the manner of a ritual'. Against
this, it might be pointed out that Milton's poem is an epic,
and that epic style has traditionally been marked by stately,
ritual movement, and that epic poets have never tried to compete for flexibility or rhythmic variety with lyricists or
dramatists.

Judgment of rhythmic quality must take account of genre,
of the kind of poem one is dealing with. The rhythms appropriate to a stirring ballad or an exciting narrative poem
would not be adequate to the purposes of a poet concerned to
trace the subtle contours of inner tension recorded in

Herbert's *Collar,* nor would Herbert's delicate modulations be at all appropriate to record what Browning has to tell in:

> I sprang to the stirrup, and Joris, and he;
> I galloped, Dirck galloped, we galloped all three . . .
> > (*How They Brought the Good News*)

In its own way, Browning's uncomplicated rhythmic pattern is as apt for its purpose (the telling of a simple, straight-forward story, involving lively activity) as is Milton's stately, sonorous verse for its purpose (the treatment of a great and momentous subject). The basic questions about rhythm, whatever the work, are ones like the following: To what extent does it help to express the feeling appropriate to the subject-matter, to what extent is it an adequate reflection of the mean-ing of the poem and of the intentions of the poet? If a poet is lamenting the death of someone dear to him, a piece of verse whose rhythms are mechanical and unvaried does not match the occasion. This is what is wrong with most of the obituary verses we find in newspapers and on memorial cards. And if an event such as Christmas is being celebrated in verse, this is not best done in rhythms as predictable as hammer-blows. For an example of how rhythms can be used expressively, con-sider the following from *Hamlet.* Claudius is speaking to his court.:

> Therefore our sometime sister, now our Queen,
> Th' imperial jointress to this warlike state,
> Have we, as 'twere, with a defeated joy,
> With an auspicious and a dropping eye,
> With mirth in funeral, and with dirge in marriage,
> In equal scale weighing delight and dole,
> Taken to wife . . .
> > (I, ii, 8)

The rhythm and movement of this speech contribute signifi-cantly to the characterisation of Claudius. The insidious and spurious balancing help to fix his persona for us. Again, con-sider Shakespeare's presentation of Macbeth's reaction after he has been greeted as Thane of Cawdor:

> This supernatural soliciting
> Cannot be ill, cannot be good. If ill,
> Why hath it given me earnest of success
> Commencing in a truth? I am Thane of Cawdor.
> If good, why do I yield to that suggestion
> Whose horrid image doth unfix my hair,
> And make my seated heart knock at my ribs
> Against the use of nature?

> > > (I, iii, 130)

What L. C. Knights calls 'the sickening see-saw rhythms' of this speech suggest the pounding heart knocking at the ribs: we get the very feel of Macbeth's experience.

Rhythm in poetry strenuously resists discussion in terms of rules or mechanical formulae. Little real purpose is served by mathematical analysis of rhythmic patterns. In successful poems, rhythm is intimately linked with feeling. The poet selects the appropriate rhythms instinctively, not as the result of calculation. One can however, record the effects and discuss the appropriateness of various kinds of rhythm, slow, measured, emphatic in poems of meditation:

> The curfew tolls the knell of parting day,
> The lowing herd wind slowly o'er the lea,
> The ploughman homeward plods his weary way,
> And leaves the world to darkness and to me . . .

or the quick, eager movement of:

> > > and then my heart
> Like to the lark at break of day arising
> From sullen earth, sings hymns at heaven's gate . . .

or the heavy rhythms, the swaying ritual movement of:

> The hasty multitude
> Admiring enter'd, and the work some praise
> And some the Architect: his hand was known
> In Heav'n by many a Towered structure hugh,
> Where Scepter'd Angels held their residence . . .

These are relatively simple examples. More subtle discriminations are a feature of good critical analysis. Examination of Donne's use of his stanza form will show how, in the words of F. R. Leavis, the exigencies of the pattern 'play an essential part in the consummate control of intonation, gesture, movement and larger rhythm' (*Revaluation*, p. 12). Donne's rhythms are in general those of the talking voice; Dryden's largely influenced by the fact that his effects are for the public ear, Milton's in *Paradise Lost* by a consciousness that he and his readers are participating in a solemn ritual exercise.

Bibliography: G. Saintsbury, *A Historical Manual of English Prosody*, 1910, Macmillan; R. M. Alden, *English Verse*, 1903, Holt; F. R. Leavis, *Imagery and Movement: Notes in the Analysis of Poetry Scrutiny*, September 1945, *Scrutiny – A Quarterly Review 1932–53*, H. Coombes, *Literature and Criticism*, 1953, Chatto; D. Thompson, *Reading and Discrimination*, 1965, Chatto 1934 and 1954, reprinted Humanities Press 1962; James McAuley, *Versification*, Michigan State University Press, 1966; G. N. Leech, *A Linguistic Guide to English Poetry*, 1969, Longmans; G. S. Fraser, *Metre, Rhyme and Free Verse*, 1970, Methuen; I. A. Richards, *Practical Criticism* (1929), paperback 1973, Routledge and Keegan Paul, 1964.

Satire

It is best to begin a description of literary satire in terms of its commonly-accepted aims and methods. Its chief aim is to diminish the status of its subject in the eyes of its readers. The satirist does this by arousing ridicule, amusement, contempt, hatred, anger, scorn, disgust or other hostile emotions. Many satirists, though by no means all, have proposed more lofty aims for themselves: the amendment of vices and the reformation of manners, for example. Whatever the aim, the classic targets of satire are folly and vice, and its field of operation is human society. The satirist is more fully conscious than most people of the contrast between the way things are and the way they ought to be; he exploits the differences that exist between appearance and reality, between what people officially stand for and how they behave, between words and deeds (see the article on Irony). It is clear that the number of possible subjects for satire is unlimited. The Roman satirist Juvenal said that satire has an interest in everything that men do. The satirist can direct his attack at an individual or type (Dryden's Shadwell), a social class or set of institutions (Pope's *Rape of the Lock*), an organisation (the English Church in Milton's *Lycidas*), a nation, or even mankind (Swift in *Gulliver's Travels*). The great majority of satirists have confined their attention to those vices and follies for which men are morally responsible, 'to what all mortals may correct' in Swift's words.

The general term 'satire' must be distinguished from the literary composition called formal satire. We find elements of satire in very many literary forms: epics, monologues, narrative poems, ballads, sonnets, pastoral poems. There are very few poetic situations in which satire cannot make an incidental appearance. Milton, following a convention of pastoral poetry, introduces scathing satire into the pastoral elegy; there are satirical passages in Chaucer's Prologue to the *Canterbury Tales* and in *Paradise Lost*. In Book III of his epic, Milton gives vent to some coarse, unsubtle satire at the expense of some practices of the Catholic church. Satan, making his way to the newly-created Earth, encounters the odd inhabitants of the Limbo of Vanities:

Embryoes and idiots, eremites and friars,
White, black and gray, with all their trumpery.
Here pilgrims roam, that strayed so far to seek
In Golgotha Him dead, who lives in heaven;
And they who, to be sure of paradise,
Dying put on the weeds of Dominic,
Or in Franciscan think to pass disguised . . .
A violent cross wind from either coast
Blows them transverse ten thousand leagues awry
Into the devious air: then might ye see
Cowls, hoods and habits with their wearers tossed
And fluttered into rags, then relics, beads,
Indulgences, dispenses, pardons, bulls,
The sport of winds: all these upwhirled aloft,
Fly o'er the backside of the world far off
Into a limbo large and broad, since called
The Paradise of Fools . . .

(474–96)

The extent and nature of Chaucer's satire in *The Canterbury Tales* are more problematical. More than three hundred lines are devoted to the description of nine ecclesiastical pilgrims. In the case of two of these, the Parson and the Clerk of Oxford, there can be no question of satire. The former is straightforwardly presented as a model of righteousness; the latter as a man devoted to scholarship and without worldly ambition. Figures like the Monk, Summoner and Pardoner are subjected to various kinds of satirical contemplation, some of it quite subtle (as in the case of the Monk). It is more difficult to be sure of the portrait of the Prioress, but it is safe to say that Chaucer did not intend his readers (frequent suggestions to the contrary notwithstanding) to condemn her as worldly, ambitious or insensitive to suffering. If there is satire at her expense, it is of the very mildest kind, and bears on her little indulgences and foibles.

Satires can very considerably in tone. They can be crude and vulgar, coarse and brutal, refined and elegant, witty and urbane, relaxed and informal, morally committed and didactic, contemptuous and indignant, amused and cynical. A. Melville Clark has a good comment on the variety of which even one form, regular verse satire, is capable: 'It fluctuates

between the flippant and the earnest, the completely trivial
and the heavily didactic; it ranges from extremes of crudity
and brutality to the utmost refinement and elegance; it
employs singly or in conjunction monologue, dialogue, epistle, oration, narrative, manners-painting, character-drawing,
allegory, fantasy, travesty, and any other vehicle it chooses;
and it presents a chameleon-like surface by using all the tones
of the satiric spectrum, wit, ridicule, irony, sarcasm, cynicism,
the sardonic and invective' (*Studies in Literary Modes*, 1946, p.
32). Within the limits of a single poem, many of these con-
flicting tones may be present. There is, for example, quite a
difference in tone between these lines from *The Rape of the
Lock:*

> And hungry judges soon the sentence sign
> And wretches hang, that jury-men may dine

and these from the same poem:

> It grieves me much (reply'd the Peer again)
> Who speaks so well should ever speak in vain

When tone is in question, it is customary to distinguish
between two broadly differing kinds of satirist, the Horatian
and the Juvenalian. The first is the witty, tolerant man of the
world who can behold human vice and folly with amused contempt; the second is the serious moralist who can find little if
anything amusing in the spectacle of human degradation and
whose indignation is always breaking through. But whether
the satirist is Horatian or Juvenalian, most readers enjoy
satire. One explanation for this was supplied by Swift when
he wrote of it as 'a sort of glass, wherein beholders do generally discover everybody's face but their own, which is the chief
reason for that kind reception it meets in the world, and that
so very few are offended with it'.

The moral function of satire is a topic which rightly attracts
a good deal of critical attention. Of the English poets, Pope
and Johnson are the outstanding moral satirists. Of both it
may be claimed that their satire finds its real justification in
the fundamental seriousness of its purpose and the soundness
and centrality of its underlying values. They are moral

satirists in a sense in which Dryden and Swift are not: two of Dryden's three main satires are political polemics; the third is an attack on a personal enemy. Swift's satire may have a serious purpose, but its effect is mainly destructive and negative. His intensities, F. R. Leavis argues, 'are intensities of rejection and negation . . . and when they most seem creative of energy are most successful in spoiling, reducing, and destroying' (*The Common Pursuit*, 1962 edn., p. 79).

Pope saw himself as teacher and moralist as well as satirist. Consider the following from the *Moral Essays:*

> Rufa, whose eye quick-glancing o'er the Park
> Attracts each light gay meteor of a Spark,
> Agrees as ill with Rufa studying Locke,
> As Sappho's diamonds with her dirty smock,
> Or Sappho at her toilet's greasy task,
> With Sappho fragrant at an evening Mask:
> So morning Insects that in muck begun,
> Shine, buzz, and fly-blow in the setting-sun . . .
> (Epistle II: *Of the Characters of Women*, 21-8)

Here physical repulsiveness acquires powerful moral implications. Sappho's moral depravity is underlined by Pope through the comparison he draws between her and an insect in its contrasted morning and evening phases. The insect simile, which takes up only a single couplet, illustrates the rich compression achieved by Pope in his mature work. The simile involves a wide range of suggestion. The muck from which the insect is born has its counterpart in Sappho's cosmetic muck; the insect emerges from the muck to shine, buzz and fly-blow in the sunset, while Sappho's 'dirty smock' gives place to her sinister fragrance at the evening mask. Sappho's nastiness, insignificance and amorality are all conveyed in a few lines. And if she shares beauty with the insect, she is likewise ephemeral.

In the Fourth Moral Essay, *The Epistle to Burlington,* we find a splendid illustration of Pope's belief that vice is essentially vulgar. His target on this occasion is the proud and greedy millionaire Timon, really the war profiteer Chandos, who seeks to exalt himself by building himself a huge baroque villa, lavishly but tastelessly decorated:

Greatness, with Timon, dwells in such a draught,
As brings all Brobdingnag before your thought.
To compass this, his building is a town,
His pond an ocean, his parterre a down:
Who but must laugh; the master when he sees,
A puny insect, shivering at a breeze

(103–8)

It is useful to distinguish satire proper from invective and lampoon and also from social comedy. Invective involves a violent attack in words upon a particular target (person or thing). It is a direct, straightforward attack, involving no resort to irony, but featuring energetic denunciation or vituperation. The principal formal literary expression of continuous invective is the lampoon, originally a drinking-song (French *lampons*, let us drink), and featuring a virulent or scurrilous attack upon an individual. A good example of invective is *A Glass of Beer* by James Stephens. Here are two stanzas:

The lanky hank of a she in the inn over there
Nearly killed me for asking the loan of a glass of beer;
May the devil grip the whey-faced slut by the hair,
And beat bad manners out of her skin for a year.

If I ask'd her master he'd give me a cask a day;
But she, with the beer at hand, not a gill would arrange!
May she marry a ghost and bear him a kitten, and may
The High King of Glory permit her to get the mange.

Stephens is writing in a hallowed Irish tradition. A talent for fluent and energetic cursing is a feature of Irish satirical and comic poetry. But 'proper satire', according to Johnson's *Dictionary,* 'is distinguished, by the generality of its reflections, from a lampoon, which is aimed at a particular person', and which is 'a personal satire, abuse, censure, written not to reform but to vex'.

The most valuable kind of distinction, perhaps, is that between direct invective or lampoon (which some people would still classify as satire but which is best considered as a separate form) and satire proper, which in its classic manifestations involves some degree of irony. The satirist who freely uses irony can remain coolly detached from his victim

and enjoy his superiority. He can pay the most effusive com-
pliments knowing all the time that the initiated reader will
translate these into insult and abuse. It is, as Dryden, one of
the great satirists, recognized, comparatively easy to write invective and lampoon, 'easy to call a man a rogue and a villain,
but hard to make a man a fool, a blockhead or a knave
without actually using any of these opprobrious terms'.
Dryden provides a striking image of the essential contrast
between the effect of satire involving irony and that of non-
ironical invective when he talks of the 'vast difference between
the slovenly butchering of a man and the fineness of a stroke
that separates head from body and leaves it standing in its
place'. Dryden's own portrait of Achitophel is mainly invective; his poem on Shadwell (*MacFlecknoe*) is more subtle satire.
The true satirist keeps cool since his activity is primarily intellectual; he conceals his emotion, and does not give vent to the
passionate outbursts of the lampooner.

The basic difference between social satire and social comedy lies in a fundamental difference of attitude. Social comedy, unlike social satire, is tolerant of human folly and
weakness. Social satire implies the condemnation of society by
reference to an ideal, but this ideal is not one that can easily
be realised, if it can be realised at all. In social comedy, on the
other hand, the ideal can be fairly easily reconciled with
reality. And whereas the writer of comedy regards laughter as
an end in itself, the satirist uses laughter as a weapon.

It has been said that the satirist's activity is primarily intellectual. It is also true that his original motive for writing satire
is anger or annoyance, or the sense that somebody or
something engaging his satiric interest is ridiculous or absurd.
But his strong original emotions are invariably modified by a
sense of his own superiority to his victims, and his contempt
for them and for what they represent. The whole point of the
exercise is to cause the victim to lose status, and the most effective method of bringing this about is to arouse contemptuous laughter at his expense. The contemptuous laughter of
satire can be an incidental element in satiric comedy, but is
generally absent from Shakespeare's romantic comedy, where
we tend to laugh with rather than at the comic characters.

Another point to make about satire is that it cannot be fair
or impartial. The satirist does not attempt to describe things

or people objectively. To be successful, he must to some extent be unfair. He must, for example, largely or totally ignore those aspects of the object of his satire which might make it in any way acceptable to the reader. This may be illustrated by reference to Dryden's satire on Shadwell (*MacFlecknoe*). One could never guess from this poem that the victim was a highly successful and reputable literary figure. On the other hand, Dryden does make a concessionary gesture towards Shaftesbury, his victim in *Absalom and Achitophel,* when he admits that he did credit to the bench ('The statesman we abhor, but praise the judge'). But this gesture only has the effect of making his previous attack on Shaftesbury all the more plausible, since his willingness to bestow some slight praise lends his censures an air of impartiality. Swift is one of the least constructive of satirists. He is writing primarily not to reform but to vex, not to educate his readers but to demolish his victims. When he claims in his own defence that 'His satire points at no defect / But what all mortals may correct' (*Verses on the Death of Dr Swift*), he seems to be taking are too genial a view of such savagely pessimistic examples as *A Modest Proposal* and Book IV of *Gulliver's Travels.*

A common effect of satire is to shatter the heroic view of life, to dispel, for example, the widely-held notion that certain men, by virtue of birth and rank, are set worlds apart from others, and that certain institutions, outward forms and ceremonies are to be regarded with awe and spoken of only with reverence. The satirist enjoys humbling the great men and institutions of this world, making traditional marks of distinction appear meaningless and hallowed customs and institutions ridiculous. Swift revels in such procedures. Here is the conclusion of his satirical elegy on the death of Marlborough:

> Come hither, all ye empty things,
> Ye bubbles rais'd by breath of Kings;
> Who float upon the tide of state,
> Come hither, and behold your fate.
> Let pride be taught by this rebuke,
> How very mean a thing's a Duke;
> From all his ill-got honours flung,
> Turn'd to that dirt from whence he sprung.

This reductive technique is a basic feature of the entire first book of *Gulliver's Travels,* where the political life of England is seen in terms of the childish activities of the Lilliputians (really the English), whose warlike propensities, capacity for mischief and maintenance of a class-system appear absurd in view of their diminutive stature. In Book II, the real English, as described by the naive Gulliver, appear to the enlightened King of Brobdingnag (Swift's mouthpiece at this point) as 'the most contemptible race of little odious vermin that nature ever suffered to crawl on the face of the earth'. In Pope's *Rape of the Lock,* the English court, whose head and members are presumed to decide the fate of nations, is seen as a place where in reality trivial people do little but gossip, backbite and exchange platitudes. Here satiric reduction finds its characteristic figure in bathos (an incongruous and witty descent from the elevated to the commonplace) the most celebrated example of which is: 'And thou great Anna, whom three realms obey / Dost sometimes counsel take and sometimes Tea' (Canto III, 7–8).

The satirist is less concerned with things in themselves as with man's attitude to them. One fact that gives him much scope is that many quite common objects and occupations have through time acquired sacred or dignified associations. The learned professions (law and medicine, for example) have an almost mystical status in the eyes of the uninitiated. It is for the satirist to destroy the symbolism associated with whatever he is concerned to diminish, often by pretending total ignorance of such symbolism, and offering a harsh version of the thing itself. Here, for example, is how Swift makes Gulliver explain the English legal profession to the Master Houyhnhnm: 'I said there was a society of men among us, bred up from their youth in the art of proving, by words multiplied for the purpose, that white is black, and black is white, according as they are paid. To this society, the rest of the people are slaves . . . My lawyer being practised almost from his cradle in defending falsehood, is quite out of his element when he would be an advocate for justice' (Book IV, Ch. V). In passages such as this, Swift breaks with common form by divorcing the trappings of the legal profession from what he conceives of as its reality, thereby depriving it of its respectability.

An effective device by means of which the satirist can

reduce the stature of his victims or destroy the symbolism widely associated with his targets is the invention of a mouthpiece or the assumption of a *persona* or mask. In Swift's most celebrated satire, Gulliver is not, except at rare moments, to be identified with the author. He is, instead, to be taken as one of the *personae* or masks assumed by Swift. Another is the King of Brobdingnag, who dominates Book II. He is one of Swift's most effective devices, his primary purpose being to undermine the status of European society in the reader's eyes. Swift makes him an honest, logical, clear-sighted commentator who sees no reason why appearances should contradict realities, why trivialities should be taken seriously and serious things trivialised. When these and other aspects of European society are described to him by Gulliver, he is at a loss to understand them, and refuses to see the symbolic meanings which Europeans attach to what seem to him absurd customs and ideas. The 'naive' character of this persona forces Gulliver to describe European life and institutions to him in primitive, almost childish terms, without ceremonial trappings, with the result that the reader is forced to see them, as Swift wants him to, in a new, often absurd and terrifying light. Thus Gulliver's account of European engines of war, which he fondly imagines will favourably impress his royal listener, in fact horrifies and revolts him, as it is meant to horrify and revolt his reader. See separate article on Irony.

Bibliography: H. Walker, *English Satire and Satirists,* 1925, Dent; D. Worcester, *The Art of Satire,* 1940, Oxford University Press; H. Davis, *The Satire of Jonathan Swift,* 1947, Macmillan, Toronto; Ian Jack, *Augustan Satire, 1660–1750,* 1952, Oxford University Press; James Sutherland, *English Satire,* 1958, Cambridge University Press; A. Kernan, *The Cankered Muse. Satire of the English Renaissance,* 1959, Oxford University Press; R. C. Elliott, *The Power of Satire,* Princeton, 1960 Princeton University Press; G. Highet, *The Anatomy of Satire,* Princeton 1962, Princeton University Press; J. Russell and Ashley Brown, ed., *Satire: A Critical Anthology,* 1967, World Publishing Company; R. Paulson *The Fictions of Satire,* 1967, Johns Hopkins Press; P. Dixon, *The World of Pope's Satires,* 1968, Methuen; M. J. C. Hodgart, *Satire,* 1969, Weidenfeld and Nicolson; A. Pollard, *Satire,* 1970, Methuen.

The Sonnet

The sonnet, or single-stanza lyric, is, in many respects, the most challenging of literary forms. Its fourteen lines are just long enough to make possible the fairly complex development of a single theme, and short enough to test the poet's gift for concentrated expression. His freedom is further restricted by a demanding rhyme-scheme, and a conventional metrical form (iambic pentameter). The greatest sonnets are those in which the poet has managed to overcome the limitations of the form, has achieved the great aim of reconciling freedom of expression, variety of rhythm, mood and tone, richness of imagery, with adherence to a rigid set of conventions. It is interesting and instructive to observe the struggle and to feel the tensions between the demands of the sonnet form and the poet's desire to give the freest possible range to his gifts. Wordsworth's account of his own experience with the sonnet is famous:

> In truth the prison, unto which we doom
> Ourselves, no prison is; and hence for me,
> In sundry moods, 'twas pastime to be bound
> Within the sonnet's scanty plot of ground;
> Pleased if some souls (for such there needs must be)
> Who have felt the weight of too much liberty,
> Should find brief solace there, as I have found . . .
> ('Nuns fret not at their convent's narrow room' . . .)

English poets have traditionally made use of one of two kinds of sonnet. The Petrarchan, favoured by Milton and Wordsworth, falls into two divisions, the octave (eight lines rhyming abba abba) and the sestet (six lines generally rhyming cde cde). The octave generally deals with a problem, situation or incident; the sestet resolves the problem or comments on the situation or incident. The Shakespearian sonnet is different, consisting of three quatrains (groups of four lines rhyming ab ab cd cd ef ef) and a rhyming couplet (gg). At times, Shakespeare partly follows the Petrarchan fashion by employing the octave-sestet thematic pattern (see Sonnets 23 and 29) but more often tends to use his three quatrains to state and develop his theme, while his rhyming couplet either clinches his argument or reverses the whole trend of the first twelve lines (Compare Sonnet 23 with Sonnet 30).

Shakespeare's sonnets are, we need hardly be reminded, the poems of a dramatist. He wrote each as he would a speech in one of his plays. The tones of the speaking voice, its rising and falling inflections, are always present. The rhyming-scheme he employs lends itself more easily to this kind of vocal composition than does that of the Petrarchan sonnet, as any sensitive reading aloud or good recording will demonstrate. Aside from their closeness to the rhythms of the speaking voice, the sonnets are dramatic in that they are conceived as varied responses to given situations, responses which reveal something of the character of the speaker. Much discussion of Shakespeare's sonnets tends to centre less on the technical and artistic achievement they represent than on their biographical implications. In a famous poem Wordsworth declared that in the sonnets 'Shakespeare unlocked his heart'. Beginning from some such premise, generations of commentators have been tempted to supplement the meagre factual information about Shakespeare's life by reading in the sonnets the record of the poet's personal relationships, his conflicts, problems and sorrows. It does not need much ingenuity to discover a 'story' in the sonnets if they are read as a sequence. We have the poet's adoration of the young friend who, along with the poet's mistress, betrays him; the rivalry between the poet and another writer (presumably George Chapman) for the patronage or affection of the young friend; the poet's farewell to the latter; his varied addresses to his mistress; his reflections on old age, death, the joys and sorrows of love, on poetic immortality, his disillusionment, his turning to religion. But it is by no means certain, even likely, that the present order of the sonnets is the correct one, or even that the collection of 154 poems is a heterogeneous whole. Against the notion that 'Shakespeare unlocked his heart' in the sonnets, it might be urged that in not all of them are his emotions very deeply engaged, and that some of them are conventional literary exercises on conventional themes. On the other hand, it is impossible to read the best and most compelling of them without being conscious that what is being said arises from deeply-felt actual experiences. The intense emotion of the sonnets on the friend's fault and on his own sense of guilt show that Shakespeare is not writing satiric or conventional exercises through the whole series. The irony of No. 94, for example, is serious and destructive, and the final couplet is extremely bitter ('For sweetest things turn sourest by their deeds / Lilies that fester, smell far worse than weeds'). Perhaps the safest general conclusion is that the Shakespeare sonnet sequence is really a miscellaneous collection, not planned as a unity, some of the sonnets being heartfelt responses to particular situations or moods (Nos. 27, 28, 116 and 148, for example); others more flippant (No. 130); others again literary exercises on commonplace themes (Nos. 55, 64 and 65).

It is important to bear in mind that Shakespeare's favourite themes are also those of a host of contemporary writers in the sonnet form, and that it is difficult to find a single Shakespeare sonnet dealing with time, decay, death, love, friendship or poetic immortality that cannot be closely paralleled in some contemporary work. This can to a large extent be accounted for by the fact that Shakespeare and his contemporaries were drawing heavily for both themes and formulations on the work of Ovid and Horace. The nature of Shakespeare's debt to these poets is well documented by J. B. Leishman in his book, *Themes and Variations in Shakespeare's Sonnets*. Some of Shakespeare's greatest sonnets deal with the theme of poetic immortality. Here are some lines by Spenser on the same theme:

> One day I wrote her name upon the strand,
> But came the waves and washed it away:
> Again I wrote it with a second hand,
> But came the tide, and made my pains his prey.
> Vain man, said she, that dost in vain assay
> A mortal thing so to immortalize:
> For I myself shall like to this decay,
> And eke my name be wiped out likewise.
> Not so, quoth I, let baser things devise
> To die in dust, but you shall live by fame:
> My verse your virtues rare shall eternize,
> And in the heavens write your glorious name,

Where, whenas death shall all the world subdue,
Our love shall live, and later life renew

(*Amoretti,* No. 75)

And here is a sonnet by Michael Drayton; the seventh and eighth lines are reminiscent of Shakespeare:

How many paltry, foolish, painted things,
That now in coaches trouble every street,
Shall be forgotten whom no poet sings,
Ere they be well wrapped in their winding-sheet!
Where I to thee eternity shall give,
When nothing else remaineth of these days,
And Queens hereafter shall be glad to live
Upon the alms of thy superfluous praise.
Virgins and matrons, reading these my rhymes,
Shall be so much delighted with thy story
That they shall grieve they liv'd not in these times,
To have seen thee, their sex's only glory.
So shalt thou fly above the vulgar throng.
Still to survive in my immortal song.

(Sonnet 6)

Shakespeare is incontestably the greatest English master of the sonnet form. The best of his sonnets have a richness of texture, a metaphorical density, an inevitable rightness of phrase, a classic perfection, to be found nowhere else. The sonnets of Milton, another great master of the form, differ fundamentally in outlook, themes and style from those of Shakespeare and his contemporaries. Many of them bear the stamp of Milton's puritanism. In contrast to the light grace, richness and ornate beauty of the Elizabethan sonnet, Milton's are distinguished by vigour, dignity and high seriousness, often by a consistent solemnity. They are less flexible and subtle than Shakespeare's, more sonorous and direct, more restrained. Wordsworth spoke of the 'republican austerity' of Milton's sonnets. Milton is generally credited with having brought about a major change in the subject-matter of the English sonnet, a change celebrated by Landor:

He caught the sonnet from the dainty hand
Of Love, who cried to lose it; and he gave
The notes to Glory. .

Only one of Milton's English sonnets deals with love, and then only in passing. Half of them are poems of friendship, the rest devoted to an attack on the Presbyterians ('*One the new forcers of conscience. .*'), an appeal for protection in time of war ('Captain or Colonel. . . .'), the defence of a pamphlet, his birthday (*On being arrived at the age of twenty-three*), his blindness, his dead wife, the Piedmontese martyrs ('Avenge O Lord . . .')

It is this extension of the subject-matter of the English sonnet that constitutes Milton's most significant contribution to the form. And the nature of his subject-matter largely determines his style. With subjects like his, the elaborate trifling, the playful ingenuity, the conceits and exaggerations of the Elizabethans could have no place. Instead of ingenuity we find seriousness, directness and simplicity. Milton tends to plunge straight into his subject, eleven of his nineteen sonnets beginning with vocatives. We gather from the sonnets not a sense of Milton's cleverness but of his sincerity and commitment. Each of them was called forth by some actual event or powerful emotion, hence, perhaps, their small number. They carry little of the stamp of conventional literary exercises. Furthermore, Milton differs from most of his predecessors in having scant respect for the traditional sonnet structure inherited from the Italian models. In most Elizabethan sonnets, the pauses at the end of the first quatrain and of the octave are preserved. In six of his sonnets, Milton omits the first pause, and in nine he omits the second. One of his best-known sonnets (*On the late Massacre in Piedmont*) illustrates his unusual freedom from conventional restraint. Nine of its fourteen lines are run-on. The sestet is not strictly separated from the octave even in sound, since the long *o* which echoes through the octave is carried on into three of the last six lines. The Italians and Elizabethans tended to avoid pauses within the line; Milton often ignores this tradition. The prosody of his sonnets is rather like that of the Blank Verse of *Paradise Lost,* featuring at times an inversion of the normal English word-order common in the epic:

> Vane, young in years, but in sage counsel old,
> Than whom a better Senator ne'er held
> The helm of Rome. . . .
>
> (Sonnet XVII)

John Donne's nineteeen *Holy Sonnets* form a group of particular importance and interest. Technically Donne is, with
the exception of Hopkins (who has much in common with
him) the most exciting of English sonneteers. A brief examination of one of the best of Donne's sonnets (*Holy Sonnet*
XIV: 'Batter my Heart, three person'd God. .') will indicate
some characteristic features of his work in the form. In the
Holy Sonnets, Donne's obsessive spiritual anxiety, his profound
agitation, find an outlet in urgent, strained phrases; rhythm
and metre are dislocated in a perfect correspondence between
subject-matter and poetic form. In *Holy Sonnet* XIX, there is a
powerful tension between the emotional excitement generated
by the theme and the structural requirements of the sonnet
form. Donne preserves the basic outline of the Elizabethan
sonnet: fourteen lines, five strong stresses to the line, division
into octave and sestet. But one is much more conscious here
than in the work of Donne's predecessors and contemporaries
of the poet's struggle to reconcile violent feeling with the strict
demands of the sonnet form. The rhythm and movement of
the first four lines enact the tremendous onslaught which is to
free the speaker from sin and make him God's prisoner. The
ferocity and speed of the attack is conveyed in a remarkable
sequence of heavily stressed verbs (batter, o'erthrow, break,
blow, burn). Donne makes telling use of the opposition
between the pauses dictated by his meaning on the one hand,
and those dictated by his verse-pattern on the other, as when
he carries over the sense from the end of one line to the beginning of the next ('for you / As yet but knock . . .'; 'for I / Except you enthral me . .'). There is a sharp contrast between
the tone and movement of lines 1–4 and lines 5–8. The
feverish activity and emotional excitement of the first four
lines with their almost bullying tone give way to the
apologetic pleading of the next four. In lines 9 and 10 the tone
changes again, and with it the metaphor: images of conflict
are replaced by those of love; demand gives way to longing. In
the final four lines there is a renewal of agitation and torment
as well as a brilliant and unexpected fusing of the earlier
metaphors of physical violence and love. Here, as elsewhere,
Donne makes the sonnet a vehicle for passionate and paradoxical argument, the demands of which govern the shape of the
poem and the choice of images. The cadences of living speech
are the bases of Donne's rhythms.

After Milton and Donne, the most notable (certainly the most dedicated) English exponent of the sonnet form was Wordsworth, who wrote more than five hundred sonnets. For a long time throughout the eighteenth century, the sonnet had been a vehicle for sentimental, melancholy musings and trivial ideas. Wordsworth, like Milton, re-dedicated it to serious purposes, and in this he was strongly influenced by Milton's example. Like Milton, Wordsworth wrote some notable sonnets on public and patriotic themes ('Milton, thou shouldst be living at this hour . .'.) and on deeply-felt private griefs (*Surprised by Joy*). Wordsworth's debt to Milton's influence extended even to technique. He conformed so closely to Milton's practice that many of his sonnets read like blank verse. Most of his sonnets are pedestrian exercises, but the best of them are among the finest in the language. *Surprised by Joy* is a challenging, profoundly disturbing and stimulating poem, demanding a sensitive vigilance from the reader, with its many shifts of tone, emphasis and modulation. F. R. Leavis has justly remarked that 'here we have deeply and finely experienced emotion poetically realized, the realization being manifested in a sensitive particularity, a delicate sureness of control in complex effects, and, in sum, a fineness of organization, such as could come only of a profoundly stirred sensibility in a gifted poet' (*Scrutiny*, September 1945, p. 127).

Not even the briefest account of the sonnet form would be complete without some reference to at least two sonnets of Keats: *On First Looking into Chapman's Homer* and *The Terror of Death* ('When I have fears that I may cease to be'). The first is one of the most perfect of all English sonnets; the second not unworthy to stand comparison with Shakespeare's highest achievements in the form for precision and density of imagery. Here is the Chapman sonnet (an overnight composition of the poet's youth):

> Much have I travelled in the realms of gold,
> And many goodly states and kingdoms seen;
> Round many western islands have I been
> Which bards in fealty to Appollo hold.
> Oft of one wide expanse had I been told
> That deep-browed Homer ruled as his demesne;
> Yet did I never breathe its pure serene
> Till I heard Chapman speak out loud and bold;

> Then felt I like some watcher of the skies
> When a new planet swims into his ken;
> Or like stout Cortez when with eagle eyes
> He stared at the Pacific, and all his men
> Looked at each other with a wild surmise –
> Silent, upon a peak in Darien.

The beauty of this sonnet, as John Fuller points out, 'lies in the brilliant risk Keats takes of anticipating his boldest image by launching straight away into metaphors of voyaging'. By the end of the octave, the theme has been fully developed, so that the sestet must take some new turn if Keats is to avoid tame repetition. Fuller argues that the last four lines succeed because 'stout Cortez' is "so specific, so far removed from the Mediterranean and so particularly appropriate figuratively to Keats's main point which is that just as Cortez (though Keats means Balboa) discovers a continent through an ocean (i.e. that he is not in Asia after all) so Keats discovers Homer through Chapman's translation. This is what the 'wild surmise' is all about: the discovery in each case is indirect" (*The Sonnet*, 1972, p. 6).

The major English sonnets since the Romantic age are those of G. M. Hopkins, whose work in the form represents a radical departure from tradition. Some of his experiments are so highly idiosyncratic that they do not point in directions which might conceivably be useful to imitators, but they mark an important stage in the development of the sonnet form. The traditional sonnet is written in iambic pentameters, which means that in each line there are ten syllables, five weak and five strong (When I have fears that I may cease to be). Hopkins introduced the notion of sprung rhythm, which dispenses with the custom of having a fixed number of syllables per line, although it does involve a fixed number of strong or stressed syllables per line. In addition to the strong stresses, Hopkins allows for some additional stresses called 'outriders' which must be adequately stressed, though not to the same extent as the strong syllables. Here is an example. The 'outriders' are *italicised*:

> Felix Ran*dal* the farr*ier,* o is he dead th*en*? My duty all
> ended.

Of the eighteen syllables in the line above there are six strong stresses, three 'outriders' and nine weak syllables. Hopkins does not use sprung rhythm in all his poems. Some of the sonnets ('No worst, there is none'; 'I wake and feel the fell of dark' and 'Thou art indeed just, Lord', for example) are written in standard rhythm. Hopkins imposes order and pattern on his poems by free use of internal rhyme and alliteration, which devices help to organize verse composed in sprung rhythm. For those who find the technicalities of sprung rhythm beyond their comprehension, an observation of Hopkins may be of help: 'Take breath and read it with the ears, as I always wish it to be read, and my verse becomes all right.' Hopkins' sprung rhythm is a very far cry from the traditional iambic pentameter, and in some sonnets (*That Nature is a Hericlitean Fire,* for example) he goes beyond the customary fourteen lines, while in others (*Pied Beauty,* for example), he falls short of the traditional length. He does, however, generally preserve the Petrarchan rhyming-scheme (abba abba cde cde) and the Petrarchan octave-sestet division.

Bibliography: J. S. Smart, *The Sonnets of John Milton,* Glasgow, 1921, Jackson; R. D. Havens, *The Influence of Milton on English Poetry,* Harvard University Press 1922, re-issue 1960 Russell and Russell; W. H Gardner, *G. M. Hopkins,* 1948, Secker and Warbeck (also Oxford University Press 1958 – see page 68 'Inscape and Instress'); J. W. Lever, *The Elizabethan Love-Sonnet,* 1956, Methuen; J. B. Leishman, *Themes and Variations in Shakespeare's Sonnets,* 1961, Hutchinson; L. C. John, *The Elizabethan Sonnet Sequences,* New York, 1964, Russell and Russell; John Fuller, *The Sonnet,* 1972, Methuen.

Symbolism

Before one talks about literary symbols and symbolism, it is well to remind oneself that words themselves are symbolic, in that they stand for something other than themselves, and in that their relationship to the things they stand for is not a necessary one, but arbitrary (different languages use widely differing words for the same object). Signs as well as words can be symbolic, provided that the relationship between the sign and what it stands for is arbitrary. This is neatly explained by C. L. Barber's account of two traffic signs: 'The first shows two children running into the road: this is not symbolic, but representational, for it gives an actual picture of the hazard ahead of the motorist, who does not need to be initiated into the meaning of the sign. The second shows a blazing torch; this stands for learning, and indicates that there is a school ahead, but the relationship between a blazing torch and learning is an arbitrary one, and the motorist needs to have its meaning explained to him; the blazing torch is a symbol' (*The Story of Language,* 1972 edn., p. 18). A parallel distinction is that between a man shaking his fist in anger (in which case the gesture is representational), and a man raising a flattened hand in a fascist salute (a symbolic gesture).

While all words are symbols, because they signify things other than themselves, literary symbolism comes about when the objects signified by the words stand in turn for things other than themselves. At a simple level, symbolism is familiar to almost everybody because certain conventional symbols are universally popular. Certain objects are commonly associated with fixed qualities or ideas: the cross with Christianity, the eagle with heroism, the rising sun with birth, the setting sun with death, the dove with peace, and so on. Certain adjectives of colour have commonly-accepted symbolic meanings: white, black, green, red, yellow, for example. This colour symbolism can be studied in such poems as Marvell's *The Garden* and Dylan Thomas' *Fern Hill.* It should be noticed that colour symbols have no fixed meaning, but derive their significance from a context: green may signify innocence or naiveté or Irish patriotism.

The point to make about symbolism as it appears in

successful symbolist works is that the literary symbol appeals to the imagination and to the instinctive feelings of the reader, not to the intellect, that it is not a token with a precise, definite, clearly established conceptual reference, to be pinned down and accurately described. Symbolism may be described as the art of expressing emotions not by describing them directly nor by defining them through overt comparisons with concrete images, but by *suggesting* what these ideas and emotions are by re-creating them in the mind of the reader through the use of unexplained symbols. These symbols help to convey a mood to the subconscious mind rather than an appeal to the rational faculties. A comparison between metaphor and symbol will help to illustrate this idea. Metaphor (in a well-known definition) is 'a word or phrase literally denoting one kind of object or idea used in place of another by way of suggesting a likeness or analogy between them'. Every metaphor has at least two fixed or assignable meanings: the meaning it literally conveys, and the other meaning it stands for or suggests. The symbol, on the other hand, has only *one* fixed meaning: its literal one. Its other meanings are far too elusive for us to be able to fix. We are free to suggest a range of reference for a symbol, provided that we bear in mind that what we suggest can only be part of its meaning, or one of its possible meanings. The key word is 'suggest'; the French symbolist poet Mallarmé is supposed to have said that he banished the words 'like' and 'as' from his vocabulary. A symbol can often be so flexible that it can have almost any meaning that an audience chooses to read into it in its context. Yeats's comment on Shelley's imagery of caves shows how resonant symbols can be, how their meanings tend to expand almost indefinitely:

'Again and again one finds some passing allusion to the cave of man's mind, or to the caves of his youth, or to the cave of mysteries we enter at death, for to Shelley . . . it is more than an image of life in the world. It may mean any enclosed life, as when it is the dwelling place of Asia and Prometheus, or when it is the 'still cave of poetry', and it may have all meanings at once, or it may have as little meaning as some ancient religious symbol enwoven from the habit of centuries with the patterns of a carpet or a tapestry . . . '

The arbitrary character of literary symbol is well conveyed

in a stanza from Hardy's *Neutral Tones*:

> Since then, keen lessons that love deceives,
> And wrings with wrong, have shaped to me
> Your face, and the God-curst sun, and a tree,
> And a pond edged with grayish leaves.

Middleton Murry's comment on these lines is worth quoting
for what it has to say on an important feature of symbolism:
"The poet declares that he concentrates a whole world of bitterness in a simple vision: the feeling of bitterness of love
shapes into a symbol; 'Your face, and the God-curst sun, and a
tree, and a pond edged with grayish leaves'. A mental process
of this kind is familiar to most people. At an emotional crisis
in their lives some part of their material surroundings seems to
be involved in their emotion; some material circumstance sud-
denly appears to be strangely appropriate, appropriate even
by its very incongruousness, to the stress of their soul; their
emotion seems to flow out and crystallize about this circumstance, so that for ever after the circumstance has the power of
summoning up and recreating the emotion by which it was
once touched. It gives to that emotion a preciseness which is
never possessed by emotions which did not find their symbol'
(*The Problem of Style*, 1922, pp. 87–8).

Symbols can be used in many ways. At one extreme, the
symbolist writer can make use of symbols so purely private,
personal and indeterminate that it is difficult for the reader to
discover what is being suggested, and even the context cannot
do much to help the symbols generate their meaning. Isolated
instances of this kind may be found in the poetry of T. S.
Eliot. In *Portrait of a Lady*, for example, we read that the lady's
voice 'returns like the insistent out-of-tune / Of a broken
violin on an August afternoon'. It is difficult to see the point of
the reference to the August afternoon; here we seem to have a
purely personal symbol, reflecting some intimate experience,
which cannot have the kind of meaning for any reader that it
had for the poet. This use of symbol is typical of the French
symbolists. The assumptions underlying the work of these
poets (who had a significant influence on Yeats and Eliot) are
discussed by Edmund Wilson:

'Every feeling or sensation we have, every moment of consciousness, is different from every other; and it is, in conse-

quence, impossible to render our sensations as we actually experience them through the conventional and universal language of ordinary literature. Each poet has his unique personality; each of his moments has its special tone, its special combination of elements. And it is the poet's task to find, to invent, the special language which will alone be capable of expressing his personality and feelings. Such a language must make use of symbols; what is so special, so fleeting and so vague cannot be conveyed by direct description, but only by a succession of words, of images, which will serve to suggest it to the reader. The Symbolists themselves, full of the idea of producing with poetry effects like those of music, tended to think of these images as possessing an abstract value like musical notes and chords. But the words of our speech are not musical notation, and what the symbols of symbolism really were, were metaphors detached from their subjects – for one cannot, beyond a certain point, in poetry, merely enjoy colour and sound for their own sake: one has to guess what the images are being applied to. And Symbolism may be defined as an attempt by carefully studied means – a complicated association of ideas represented by a medley of metaphors – to communicate unique personal feelings.'

(*Axel's Castle*, 1961 edn., p. 24)

Many of the symbols used in English 'symbolist' poetry (Blake, Yeats, Eliot) are essentially private tokens whose 'inward' meanings have to be reconstructed for readers by specialist scholars whose findings depend on elaborate cross-reference, and on evidence external to the poems. Eliot's garden symbolism (which includes fountains, flowers, birds and other things associated with gardens) is highly complex in its range of possible suggestion, and can never have the precise significance for the reader that it must have had for the poet. Yeats's towers, birds and beasts present similar difficulties. But most symbols are not so private and personal as to leave the reader at a loss. Many are close enough to being conventional, and many are able to generate some appropriate meanings in their contexts. In Blake's poetry, for instance, the north comes to stand for reason, the south for desire, the east for wrath, the west for pity. A good number of Blake's other symbols carry a not unexpected range of meanings or significances. Children, sheep, wild birds, wild flowers, spring, dawn and dew are innocence symbols; lions, tigers, wolves, eagles, sun fire, swords are symbols of creative, heroic energy; secrecy, hypocrisy, snakes and cities are corruption symbols, and so on. For Wordsworth, nature is a language, a system of symbols. The rocks, the crags, the streams on Simplon Pass 'Were all like workings of one mind, the features / Of the same face, blossoms upon one tree / Characters of the Great Apocalypse / The types and symbols of Eternity' (*Prelude*, VI, 1163ff). In Eliot's poetry, deserts and dust symbolize dryness of the spirit, from which water symbolizes relief. Fire is a symbol both of the burning away of corruption and of purifying grace (a traditional religious use of the fire symbol). In some of George Herbert's poems, natural familiar objects, without losing their familiar character, have rich symbolic meanings. In the following stanzas from *Vertue*, the rose is a real flower as well as a symbol of life rooted in death:

> Sweet rose, whose hue angry and brave
> Bids the rash gazer wipe his eye
> Thy root is ever in its grave
> And thou must die.

There is a large symbolic element in Shakespeare's greater plays, much of it visual. An example from *Macbeth* is the 'child crowned, with a tree in his hand' who utters the prophecy about Birnam wood coming to Dunsinane hill. The tree is a symbol of the fruitful line of Banquo's succession, and also of the 'leafy screen' which will be carried by Macbeth's advancing enemies, itself a compelling visual symbol of the tide of nature flowing over Macbeth and bringing renewal and hope to Scotland. A more general symbolic significance is made possible by Shakespeare's implicit acceptance of 'the Elizabethan world picture'. This point is well put by John Wain: 'The Renaissance mind saw three interlacing kinds of order; order within the universe; order within the political commonwealth; order within the human system. These three were in a relationship essentially analogical. The universe was a vast series of mirrors. What went on in one sphere was paralleled in the others. Not in the simple sense that cause in one sphere was immediately followed by effect in another, but in the analogical sense that the introduction of disorder at any point was a surrender, an admission of the power of the destructive principle, which constituted a general threat. Thus when Shakespeare shows Lear as committing a terrible act of political and human destructiveness, breaking up his realm and also renouncing his daughter, he naturally follows it by making him go mad (disruption of order within the human mind and body) amid a raging storm (disruption of order within the natural elements). Not that Shakespeare imagined in any naive literal way that whenever a king went mad the heavens obliged with thunder and lightning. Of course they sometimes did, and this was taken as a very natural omen. But Shakespeare's thinking on these matters was what we should call symbolic. The storm in *Lear* is like the sudden outbreak of unnatural events on the night Duncan is murdered by Macbeth' (*The Living World of Shakespeare*, 1964, p. 145).

A famous English poem whose effect depends much on the successful use of symbolism is Coleridge's *Ancient Mariner*. Some of the implications are discussed by Graham Hough: 'Untramelled progress and untried success are symbolised by the beginning of the voyage, and the albatross following the ship seems to stand for the power of nature blessing the endeavour. Then, quite wantonly, and for no reason, the Mariner kills the albatross. The sympathy between nature and the voyagers is broken, and the other sailors know and feel it . . . The death-fires dance about the ship at night and the water assumes strange and unnatural colours. The passage and what follows is a powerful symbol of a life cut off by a paralyzing sense of guilt from all sympathetic natural forces . . . The reign of life-in-death is more terrible than that of death . . . It is a complete paralysis of the will, symbolized by the motionlessness of the ship . . . The Mariner watches the water snakes in the sea; formerly they had been slimy things, symbols of horror, but now they begin to assume a strange kind of beauty. At this moment his whole feeling towards them changes: because they are alive and beautiful he blesses them. A new peace comes into his heart and he is able to sleep again. The misery and sterility of the preceding period has been symbolized by drought; and now it rains . . . What happens to him when he blesses the water-snakes in the tropical calm is a psychic rebirth – a rebirth that must happen to all men and all cultures unless they are to dry up in a living death' (*The Romantic Poets,* 1958 edn., pp. 60–3). Another critic, R. P. Warren, has also proposed a symbolic interpretation of *The Ancient Mariner,* arguing that the poem implies the concept of 'sacramentalism', the holiness of nature and all natural beings, and that it is organised on symbols of moonlight and sunlight, wind and rain.

W. B. Yeats in his critical work proposes many useful distinctions between symbolism and allegory. In an essay on Spenser he writes: 'I find that though I love symbolism, which is often the only fitting speech for some mystery of disembodied life, I am for the most part bored by allegory, which is made, as Blake says, by the daughters of memory, and coldly, with no wizard frenzy'. Graham Hough glosses the Yeatsian view of the symbolism/allegory antithesis as follows: 'Symbolism is the only possible expression of some otherwise inexpressible spiritual essence, while allegory is an arbitrary translation of some principle that is already familiar, of something that has already been expressed in other terms. So that allegory is a bucket, from which you can get no more than has been put in, while symbolism is fed by an inexhaustible spring' (*The Last Romantics,* 1947, p. 228).

See separate article on Allegory.

Bibliography: Arthur Symonds, *The Symbolist Movement in Literature,* 1900, Heinemann; Edmund Wilson, *Axel's Castle,* 1935, Scribners; C. M. Bowra, *The Heritage of Symbolism,* 1943, Macmillan; Philip Wheelwright, *The Burning Fountain, a Study in the Language of Symbolism,* 1954, Indiana University Press; G. Williamson, *A Reader's Guide to T. S. Eliot,* 1955, Thames and Hudson; W. Y. Tindall, *The Literary Symbol,* 1955, Oxford University Press; H. Levin, *Contents of Criticism,* 1957, Oxford University Press; N. Frye, *Anatomy of Criticism,* 1957, Oxford University Press; I. C. Hungerland, *Poetic Discourse,* 1958, University of California Press; J. Unterecker, *A Reader's Guide to W. B. Yeats,* 1959, Thames and Hudson; V. de Sola Pinto, *Crisis in English Poetry 1880–1940,* 1951/1968 Hutchinson; J. Unterecker, *Yeat's, A Collection of Critical Essays,* New York, 1963, Prentice-Hall, T. R. Henn, *The Lonely Tower,* 1965, Methuen; F. A. C. Wilson, *W. B. Yeates and Tradition,* 1958, Gollancz; C., Chadwick, *Symbolism,* 1971, Methuen; J. E. Cirlot, *A Dictionary of Symbols,* 1972, Routledge.

Tone

When one is trying to describe the tone of a poem, it is best to think of every poem as a spoken rather than a written exercise. A poem, then, has at least one speaker, who is addressing himself to somebody or something. In some poems, the speaker can be thought of as meditating aloud, talking to himself: we, the readers, catch him in the act and overhear him. Milton's sonnets 'How Soon Hath Time' and 'When I consider', and Keats's 'When I have fears' are examples. In other poems, the speaker is addressing himself directly to a person or object within the context of the poem. The speakers in Donne's 'Batter My Heart' and Milton's 'Avenge O Lord' are both talking to God; in Wordsworth's *Tintern Abbey* the speaker is addressing his sister; in Shelley's *Ode to the West Wind* the wind is being addressed, and so on. In dramatic poems, the speakers often reveal themselves in monologues, some of which presuppose a second fictitious person as listener (Browning's *My Last Duchess*), while in others the single speaker is addressing himself or a projection of himself (Eliot's *Prufrock*). Again, some dramatic poems may be in the form of dialogues. Herbert's *The Collar* is unusual in that it enacts a dramatic conflict between the heart and will of one speaker, who assumes two different voices. Finally, there are cases in which the speaker is neither meditating aloud nor addressing himself to an imaginary character or object within the poem, but speaking directly to the reader or listener. Dryden and Pope do this in their satires; Yeats's *September 1913* is a direct address to a certain category of listener whom the speaker clearly despises.

Each of the kinds of speaker discussed above must inevitably have an attitude to the person or object he is addressing or talking about; he must also see himself in some relationship with that same person or object. This attitude and relationship will determine the tone of his utterance. Tone, in other words, may be defined as the expression of a literary speaker's attitude to, and relationship with, his listener or his subject. In real life, one person's attitude to

163

another is often revealed in the tone of voice he adopts when he is speaking to him, and in his choice of words. At times, these things can be extremely subtle. But a sensitive reading aloud of most poems will soon reveal the tone of the speaker's utterance. The opening lines of Yeats's *September 1913* are ironical and contemptuous in tone; in *Tintern Abbey*, the speaker addresses his sister in tones of love and admiration; he talks of nature in solemn, prayerful, reverent tones, in phrases borrowed from works of Christian piety. The tone of Dryden's satiric piece on Shadwell (*Mac Flecknoe*) is one of ironic contempt; that of his portrait of Achitophel one of open hostility. In the sonnet, 'When I consider how my light is spent', Milton's tone changes from querulousness to resignation. Marvell's poem *The Garden* accommodates a wide range of tones. The opening stanza is lighthearted in its witty dismissal of the efforts of ambitious men who drive themselves to distraction in the hope of winning decorative leafy crowns, whereas if they were sensible and took their ease in a garden they might enjoy the shelter of all leaves and all trees. The second stanza is more serious and exalted in tone, without being pompous. From then on to stanza VII, there are further subtle changes in tone. Stanza VII is ecstatically happy as the soul, bird-like, prepares for its flight towards God. In Stanza VIII there is a marked lowering of tone, a shift from the awe and reverence of the previous stanza to witty, commonplace punning.

Questions of tone play a major part in modern discussions of poetry. T. S. Eliot's attempt to define the 'balance and proportion of tones' which lends Marvell's poetry its distinctive quality gave a decided impetus to other investigations of the same kind in respect of a wide variety of poets and periods. A key term in Eliot's discussion of Marvell's poetry is wit, which involves 'a recognition, implicit in the expression of every experience, of other kinds of experience which are possible'. It is this recognition and its expression that give the best of Marvell's poetry its urbane tone, its freedom from emotional extremes. Marvell addresses the discriminating reader in tones which suggest that he places a high valuation on his intelligence and sensitivity.

Consideration of tone is particularly rewarding in the case of a poet such as George Herbert, whose work displays the well-bred ease of manner of the gentleman. Herbert's calm, unruffled, well-mannered exposition of his themes is in sharp contrast to Donne's frequently aggressive, insistent, sometimes violent approach, even to God. Herbert's polite tone, his exquisite tact, is nowhere more clearly revealed than in *Love bade me welcome*, where he treats the theme of the soul's acceptance of God's love in terms of courtesy and good manners. Love (or God) is made to use the graceful modes of address of the gentlemanly host; the speaker responds in terms of the same polite code. A momentous subject is treated with delicacy and discretion; only the lines 'Ah my deare / I cannot look on thee' suggest the intensity of the feeling underlying the urbane exchanges. Herbert's fastidious taste, his preservation of decorum, may be contrasted with Robert Southwell's treatment of a similar theme in *Peter's Complaint*:

> At sorrow's door I knocked; they craved my name;
> I answered one, unworthy to be known;
> What one, say they? one worthiest of blame.
> But who? a wretch, not Gods, nor yet his own.
> A man? O no, a beast; much worse: what creature?
> A rock: how called? the rock of scandal, Peter.

The tone of this is strident and self-abasing to the point of embarrassment. Southwell is tactless and insensitive compared to Herbert, whose gentle tone of polite yet sincere self-deprecation seems absolutely appropriate.

Failures of tone similar to Southwell's can sometimes occur when personal bitterness, extreme indignation or some other emotion indulged in to excess causes a poet to lose control. This happens at times in the poetry of Shelley, whose lapses into self-pity strike a jarring note ('I fall upon the thorns of life, I bleed . . .') and whose characteristic pathos is, as F. R. Leavis remarked, 'self-regarding, directed upon an idealized self'. More extreme failures of tone can occur in patriotic poems. Consider the following not unrepresentative lines from the *Lament for the Death of Eoghan Ruadh O'Neill*, by Thomas Davis:

May God wither up their hearts! May their blood cease to
    flow!
May they walk in living death who poisoned Owen Roe

This is an extreme example of failure to achieve Eliot's ideal of 'equipoise, the balance and proportion of tones'. The result is embarrassing. That patriotic poems can preserve a balance and proportion of tones is clearly demonstrated in Yeats's *Easter 1916*. Marvell's *Horatian Ode Upon Cromwell's Return from Ireland* is another example. Marvell admires Cromwell and his achievements, but his sense of Cromwell's greatness is balanced by a recognition of his destructiveness. Marvell is officially anti-Royalist, as is his poem, yet he can present the execution of the King in these terms:

> He nothing common did or mean
> Upon that memorable scene. . .
> But bowed his comely head
> Down as upon a bed . . .

Verse satire, like patriotic poetry, can encompass a wide variety of tones: anger, earnestness, sarcasm, irony, wit, urbanity, mockery, indignation, contempt, hatred, amused tolerance. The two great Roman satirists, Horace and Juvenal, have given their names to two major kinds of satire. In the Horatian kind, the speaker maintains a tolerant, urbane attitude to his subject. He is, on the whole, amused rather than horrified, indignant or disgusted at the spectacle of human folly and vice. Pope is the great English satirist in this kind. Other eighteenth-century satirists, Swift and Johnson for example, write in the Juvenalian tradition. Johnson's two great verse satires, *London* and *The Vanity of Human Wishes,* are free imitations of Juvenal, serious, gloomy reflections on manners and mortality:

> There none are swept by sudden fate away
> But all whom hunger spares, with age decay
> Here malice, rapine, accident conspire,
> And now a rabble rages, now a fire. . . .
>
> (*London*)

And with the urbane, if still deadly, tones of Pope's personal satires, contrast the dismissive contempt of Swift's comment on the death of Marlborough:

This world he cumber'd long enough;
He burnt his candle to the snuff;
And that's the reason, some folks think
He left behind so great a stink.
(*A Satirical Elegy on the Death of a Late famous General*)

Modern emphasis on tone in English literary criticism owes much to the remarks of I. A. Richards on the meaning of poetry in his book *Practical Criticism* (1929). 'The all important fact for the study of literature', Richards argues, 'is that there are several kinds of meaning. . . . whether we are active, as in speech or writing, or passive, as readers or listeners, the total meaning we are engaged with is, almost always, a blend, a combination of several contributory meanings of different types'. Language as it is used in poetry, he argues, has several tasks to perform simultaneously, and he distinguishes four types of function, four kinds of meaning, on the basis that most human utterances can be regarded from four points of view: sense, feeling, tone and intention. Richards remarks on tone as follows: 'The speaker has ordinarily an attitude to his listener. He chooses or arranges his words differently as his audience varies, in automatic or deliberate recognition of his relation to them. The tone of his utterance reflects his awareness of this relation, his sense of how he stands towards those he is addressing' (*Practical Criticism*, p. 182).

Bibliography: I. A. Richards, *Principles of Literary Criticism*, 1928, Keegan Paul; *Practical Criticism*, 1929, Keegan Paul; T. S. Eliot, *Selected Essays*, 1932, Faber; H. Coombes, *Literature and Criticism*, 1953, Chatto; D. Thompson, *Reading and Discrimination*, 1954, Chatto; Geoffrey Walton, *Metaphysical to Agustan*, 1955, Bowes and Bowes; A. Alvarez, *The School of Donne*, 1961, Chatto; J. O. Perry, ed., *Approaches to the Poem*, 1965, Chandler Publishing; C. B. Cox and A. E. Dyson, *Modern Poetry: Studies in Practical Criticism*, 1963; E. Arnold, *The Practical Criticism of Poetry*, 1965. E. Arnold.

Tragedy

This article deals with tragic drama; illustrations are taken mainly from Shakespeare's tragedies. Tragic drama is a ritual enactment of man's consciousness of the ultimate threat to individual and social well-being by the random operation of external forces (fate, accident) and human weakness (vice, folly, error, blindness, stupidity). In tragedy we normally see a protagonist moving from positive purpose through intense suffering (an inescapable accompaniment of the tragic situation) and questioning, to awareness and perception. The events of a tragedy must be probable in sequence. The direction of the protagonist's movement is from prosperity to adversity. This is well expressed by Chaucer's Monk:

> Tragedy means a certain kind of story,
> As old books tell, of those who fell from glory,
> People that stood in great prosperity
> And were cast down out of their high degree
> Into calamity and so they died.
> (*The Canterbury Tales,* modernised by
> Nevill Coghill, 1951, p. 212)

The sequence of actions (they must be significant ones, of the kind men are constitutionally liable to perform, thus expressive of human nature) accompanying the passage of the hero from good to bad fortune is generally seen as the product of some initial and fundamental 'error' (flaw, false step, miscalculation, defect of character, misjudgment) on his part. The 'error' in question does not necessarily involve a *moral* failing. Indeed, in one of the greatest of all tragedies, the *Oedipus* of Sophocles, the hero is eventually doomed as a result of his efforts to *avoid* committing an offence against the moral law. Macbeth's initial 'fault', on the other hand, the source of all that is to happen to him, is fundamentally a moral one. It lies in the failure of his will to control the incitements to evil which so powerfully affect his imagination. His terrified question, 'Why do I yield to that suggestion / Whose horrid image

168

doth unfix my hair?' (I, iii, 133) makes the point. The 'suggestion' here is the temptation to murder. It nevertheless remains true that Macbeth's 'error' is committed in ignorance of its *full* consequences for himself.

Tragic writers are not concerned with preserving a sense of proportion between the tragic act of the protagonist and its consequences. Macbeth sins greatly against the social and moral order of his world, and opens the way for the entrance of appalling and universal forces of destruction. There is a sense in which his act and its consequences are not wholly disproportionate. By contrast, Lear's initial tragic act is foolish rather than wicked, but its ultimate issue is social and moral choas, a state of affairs where men and women become predatory monsters. Macbeth's comment on Duncan's 'gashed stabs' which 'looked like a breach in Nature / For ruin's wasteful entrance' (II, iii, 111) is powerfully expressive of the unpredictable consequences of the original tragic act. The breach or gap in nature (man's social and moral order) opened by the protagonist may be comparatively great (as in Macbeth's case), or comparatively small (as in Lear's), but once the gap is opened, the destruction wrought by the evil forces which enter through the breach can be boundless. In Shakespearian tragedy, the responsibility for opening the breach is not always the protagonist's. Hamlet, for example, is overwhelmed by the evil processes that have been activated by his uncle, and he himself becomes the agent of further ruin. H. D. F. Kitto suggests that the conception uniting the character in *Hamlet* in one coherent catastrophe is that 'evil, once started on its course, will so work as to attack and overthrow impartially the good and the bad . . . crime leads to crime, or disaster to disaster . . . it spreads from soul to soul, as a contagion, as when Laertes is tempted by Claudius, or, most notably, when, by his mother's example and Polonius' basely inspired interference, Hamlet's love is corrupted into lewdness, or when he turns against his two compromised friends and pitilessly sends them to death' (*Form and Meaning in Drama,* 1960 edn., pp. 330 ff).

An important tragic requirement is status in the protagonist. The essential features here are moral stature and greatness of personality. In Shakespearian tragedy, such qualities are invariably associated with eminent people

(Chaucer's men of 'high degree') engaged in great events. It is essential that the tragic hero be a man who can command our earnest good will, a man whose fortunes are of active and compelling interest and concern to us. He is not necessarily virtuous or free from profound guilt (Macbeth is neither). His ethical standing is of less importance than his purpose. The presentation must be such that we can identify ourselves with him in his sufferings; he must be a man who reminds us strongly of our humanity, whom we can accept as standing for us. The tragic hero must be vulnerable to extreme suffering: the relative absence of this kind of vulnerability makes Shakespeare's Richard III a doubtfully tragic figure. Failure on the dramatist's part to obtain sympathy for the tragic sufferer is crippling. The significance of status in the tragic protagonist is well underlined by Northrop Frye, who reminds us that 'tragic heroes are so much the highest points in their human landscape that they seem the inevitable conductors of the power about them, great trees more likely to be struck by lightning than a clump of grass' (*The Anatomy of Criticism*, 1957, p. 207).

The tragic protagonist meets with final and impressive disaster due to an unrealised or unforeseen failure. The false step which sets the tragic process in motion is *consciously* undertaken, but without any intention on the hero's part of bringing about the evil result which must inevitably follow for him. The notion of blindness is appropriate to his condition at this stage, just as that of rediscovered sight is appropriate to his later recognition of what he had done and what he has become as a result. A further point about the protagonist's tragic error is that once he commits it its consequences cannot be undone. When he decides to murder Duncan and usurp the throne, Macbeth deprives himself of his freedom: his life follows a determined and inescapable pattern after the fatal act.

Central to tragic plot is the process known as reversal, which is what happens when the protagonist's actions are found to have consequences the direct opposite to what he meant or expected. In tragedy, as has already been said, the protagonist moves from positive purpose through suffering to awareness. But the upshot, as Horatio expresses it in the final scene of *Hamlet*, is that we find 'purposes mistook / Fall'n on the inventors' heads' (V, ii, 376). The idea of purposes recoiling on the heads of their inventors is expressed with equal clarity in *Macbeth:* 'that we but teach / Bloody instructions, which, being taught, return / To plague the inventor' (I, vii, 8). In their blindness, both the Macbeths believe that if they usurp Duncan's throne they will be happy; what they actually achieve is almost total misery culminating in ruin. The Captain's 'So from that spring whence comfort seemed to come / Discomfort swells' (I, ii, 27) is an appropriate motto for this aspect of tragedy.

To explore the idea of reversal in tragedy it is necessary to take account of two further and closely-related features associated with the process. The tragic reversal is commonly the result of human failing and/or the workings of fate. It invariably involves tragic irony. This arises when a character acts in a manner quite inappropriate to his actual circumstances, or expects the opposite of what fate holds in store for him, or says something that anticipates the actual outcome, but not at all in the way that he means it. The most profound tragedy is that which makes free use of this tragic irony or irony of fate, where the hero's destruction is the work of his own unwitting hands or of somebody who wishes him well, where the reversal is a working in blindnesss to self-defeat. *Macbeth* is such a tragedy. The main irony for Macbeth is the ambiguous nature of the witches' prophecies on which he so confidently relies for so long. He discovers their deceptiveness too late: 'And be these juggling fiends no more believed / That palter with us in a double sense' (V, vii, 48). A major local irony is found in the scene where he goes to the witches for reassurance; what he gets instead, without realising it, is an exact forecast of the manner of his defeat and death (IV, i). What we learn from Macbeth's fate is a tragic truth about life: that men are commonly ruined not by blind chance or destiny but by their own actions or by the actions of those who wish them well. Life, as well as literature, confronts us with countless examples of men who laboriously destroy either themselves or the sources of their happiness. These actions become more tragic (and more ironic) when a man performs them, as Macbeth does, in blind ignorance of their real significance for himself.

The problem of the relative importance of fate and human

responsibility in bringing about the reversal in tragedy is an extremely knotty one. Discussion often tends to result in the formulation of maddening paradoxes. In many tragedies it is difficult to escape the impression that fatal circumstances are working against the hero from the beginning, and that whatever he may do he is in some sense a doomed man. The influence of reason, order and justice is extremely limited. A. C. Bradley expressed this idea admirably when he argued that we fail to receive an essential part of the tragic effect unless we feel at times that the tragic hero and others 'drift struggling to destruction like helpless creatures borne on an irresible flood towards a cataract; that, faulty as they may be, their fault is far from being the sole or sufficient cause of all they suffer; and that the power from which they cannot escape is relentless and unmovable' (*Shakespearean Tragedy*, 1965 edn., p. 19).

A useful way to grasp the notion of tragic inevitability is to see it in terms of the world in which the dramatist places his hero, and in which the latter must face his tragic situation. It is the dramatist's task to create this world and to organize this situation in such a way that the chances of a happy outcome are nil. Most tragedies begin with foreboding; the earliest expectation aroused is one of misfortune, and all accidents are unfortunate ones. If we could seriously feel that, in the light of all the data supplied by the drama, a more hopeful ending was quite possible and artistically acceptable, then we would not be dealing with genuine tragedy. In Oscar Mandel's admirable definition, inevitability is made the *sine qua non* of all tragedy. Mandel argues that a work of art is tragic if it substantiates the following situation: 'A protagonist who commands our earnest good will is impelled in a given world by a purpose or undertakes an action, of a certain seriousness and magnitude; and by that very purpose or action, subject to that same given world, necessarily and inevitably meets with grave spiritual or physical suffering' (*A Definition of Tragedy*, 1961, p. 20). The laws of Mandel's given world are such that in it the hero's proceedings are inseparable from disaster.

To accept all this as applying to Macbeth is not inconsistent with the claim that Shakespeare allows his hero at least a minimal and initial free will, even though his first tragic act sets off a train of events leading to disaster, and what follows from this act is made to appear beyond human control. However strong the sense of inevitability, human action is a central fact in Macbeth's tragedy. It would be absurd to argue that Shakespeare makes us see Macbeth's lapse into crime as primarily the effect of witchcraft, or wants us to believe that only the limitless influence they exert over his mind could make him act in a way totally contrary to his natural disposition. He is not *shown* as being powerless to resist the various incitements to murder, nor does the play give us a sense of his initial action being forced upon him by some unseen power. It is interesting to note that Sir Laurence Olivier portrayed him as a man 'paralysed with guilt before the curtain rises, having already killed Duncan again and again in his mind. Far from recoiling and popping his eyes, he greets the air-drawn dagger with sad familiarity; it is a fixture in the crooked furniture of his brain' (Kenneth Tynan, *Curtains*, 1961, p. 98). The most that one can say of the witches' influence is that it is considerable; there is no suggestion that he is not free to reject it. They beckon him towards a coure of action which he has probably already contemplated, however vaguely (see I, iii, 134–42). The thought of murder originates with him, not with them. They do not suggest that he should hasten the fulfilment of the prophecies by having recourse to action, evil or otherwise. The idea is his own, and he is never in a position to shift responsibility for his acts entirely to their shoulders. It is significant that the witches do not advise any course of action until long after he has already committed himself to evil. Only after he has had Banquo murdered do they tell him to be 'bloody, bold and resolute' (IV, i, 79).

In the case of *Macbeth*, then, the formula that tragedy exhibits the omnipotence of an external fate will not work. However limited we find the power of human effort against whatever forces impel men to make their unfortunate choices, we must face the fact that in this play, as in many other tragedies, fate becomes external to the hero 'only *after* the tragic process has been set going' (Frye, op. cit., p. 209). It appears that the best one can advance by way of a formula to describe the process of reversal in tragedy is to say that a combination of error of judgment and fate (in whatever proportions) is involved. The tragedies of Macbeth, Hamlet, Lear and Othello result in the placing of particular kinds of men in particular sets of circumstances. Their human limitations and a fateful conjunction of events work against them to their destruction.

Plot reversal is an essential formal element in tragedy, but discovery or recognition is often regarded as the essential tragic experience. Reversal may be seen as a means to the end of recognition, which comes to the hero through physical and mental suffering. It is the process through which he recognises his character, and becomes aware of the part he has played in bringing about the doom which his tragic purpose or action necessarily entails. Suffering alone, without recognition, is not fully tragic. Suffering and recognition (or knowledge) in tragedy must be considered together. The degree of tragic experience involved in suffering depends on the degree of knowledge it yields. The more the tragic hero (the principal focus of tragic suffering) understands his own character and situation, the greater will be his suffering. A summary of what happens in *Macbeth* could make the play look like an exciting crime story, but it is what happens *within* the hero, the development of his understanding of himself and his plight, and his sharing of this with the audience, that lifts it to a higher plane. When the unexpected results of his actions emerge, the tragic hero questions what has happened to him, and through this questioning learns the vital truth about himself. This brings him around to facing his destiny and completing it by his death. It is through recognition that he reaches his tragic vision. His error was committed in blindness; recognition involves the intrusion of the light, the acknowledgment of the blindness. Recognition is not simply his knowledge of what has happened to him (in Macbeth's case that he has been duped by the witches; in Lear's that he has been duped by his evil daughters). It also involves the new awareness of the unalterably fixed pattern of the miserable life he has created for himself through his deeds, accompanied by a profound sense of loss atthe thought of what he has sacrificed and forsaken. These elements are present in Macbeth's infinitely poignant soliloquy:

> I have liv'd long enough: my way of life
> Is fall'n into the sere, the yellow leaf;
> And that which should accompany old age,

As honour, love, obedience, troops of friends,
I must not look to have; but in their stead,
Curses not loud but deep, mouth-honour, breath
Which the poor heart would fain deny, and dare not.

(V, iii, 22)

Macbeth arrives at the recognition of having irrecoverably
lost, through his own blind deed, the things on which his happiness on earth depended. He discovers that he cannot arrest
the processes he has set in motion, and gains an insight into
the workings of evil. He realises that evil isolates and that his
deeds have cut him off from all he treasures. He is alone in a
hell of despair, and is aware of the futility of all he has planned. It is the fate of the tragic hero to be finally isolated from
the ways of men, but it is in his isolation that he grows both in
stature and self-awareness, and consequently in the estima-
tion of audience, as he faces up to his destiny and confronts it.
For Macbeth, this means dying valiantly in battle (V, ii, 32;
V, v, 52) rather than taking his own life (V, vi, 30) or running
away (V, vii, 1), or being taken prisoner (V, vii, 56).

There are various degrees of recognition in tragedy. In
Othello, for example, recognition is minimal: the protagonist
learns what he has done and what he has lost, but learns little
or nothing about himself. At the other extreme we find
tragedies – those involving martyr-saints, for example – in
which there is almost total recognition on the protagonist's
part even at the beginning; where there is little for him to discover about himself or his predicament. In *Murder in the
Cathedral,* Thomas has to learn only that he must leave himself
in God's hands. *Hamlet* has affinities with Eliot's play in this
respect; a major recognition comes in I, v, and Hamlet, like
Thomas Becket, sees himself as an instrument of providence
at the close. *Macbeth* lies somewhere between the extremes
represented by *Othello* and *Murder in the Cathedral.* By the close,
the hero's recognition is considerable, but still far from complete. There remains to the end a degree of bafflement and
wonder in his response. He is puzzled to the last, failing to
grasp the how and why of his fate. How can he understand
why he met the weird sisters and why they chose *him* to deliver
their prophecies to?

In Macbeth's case it is interesting to note that partial

recognition comes comparatively early in the play, that disillusionment sets in long before his fortunes fail, in fact when
he is at the height of his worldly success. Even before Banquo's murder, he can face the prospect of having damned his
soul ('mine eternal jewel / Given to the common enemy of
man', II, i, 67). But if he does sense early on what is happening to him as a result of what he has done, he does not really
know what kind of future is in store for him until the point at
which he realises that it is as easy for him to go forward in
crime as to go back. The recognition that he cannot control
the processes he has set in motion, or alter the course he has
set himself, is a tragic one: 'I am in blood / Stepp'd in so far
that, should I wade no more / Returning were as tedious as go
o'er' (III, iv, 136). But the exact moment when Macbeth
realises he is doomed is when Macduff relates that he was
'from his mother's womb / Untimely ripp'd' (V, vii, 44). He
has expressed an earlier, partial recognition of his fate at the
news that Birnam wood is moving towards Dunsinane (V, v,
42). It is the quality of his response to his destiny and the
manner in which he confronts it that determines his essential
worth as a tragic hero, and gives him his ultimate tragic
status. The physical death of the tragic hero is a final symbol
of his recognition; of the death of his former blind and ignorant self.

There are three basic ways of looking at tragedy. We can
examine the tragic implications of the events; the tragic experiences of the protagonist; and the effect of these on the
minds and emotions of the audience. The first two elements
have been considered above. Some comments on the third
aspect are called for. In no discussion of our response to
tragedy can we avoid reference to Aristotle's famous account
of the subject, if only because of the vast influence this account
still exercises on the minds of those who speak and write
about tragedy. In his *Poetics,* Aristotle laid down that the
primary emotions aroused by the incidents of tragedy are pity
and fear, and that our experience of tragedy involves the
'purgation' of these emotions. It is not clear whether Artistotle
meant that pity and fear are eliminated from our systems as a
result of our experience of tragic spectacle, or whether they
are purged of their impure elements. A common interpretation is that Aristotle believed that the emotions of pity and

fear are expelled as if by a medicinal purge through their very excitement in the drama, and that the spectator, to use Milton's words, 'with peace and consolation is dismissed / And calm of mind all passion spent' (*Samson Agonistes*, 1757–8).

However one interprets Aristotle's formulation, many commentators agree that the primary tragic emotions are pity and fear, and that most tragedies tend to leave the audience not depressed but relieved, even exalted. A. C. Bradley, in his classic study of Shakespearian tragedy, wrote of four responses to tragedy: a feeling of acquiescence in the catastrophe, pity, fear, and a sense of waste which the struggle, suffering and fall of the tragic figures evoke (Bradley, op. cit., p. 26). Pity is felt for the human sufferer, since he is one like ourselves; fear is experienced at his fate. In many accounts, the basis of tragic fear is seen as the 'secret cause' or fate which directs circumstances independently of human will. But it will not really do to try to sum up our response to tragedy in terms of any neat and tidy formula, even one proposed by Aristotle (whose views were based on the examination of a comparatively small number of works). Pity and fear as well as relief and a sense of waste are all likely responses to tragedy, as are clusters of related feelings ranging around these. Milton, in his Preface to *Samson Agonistes,* wrote of the purgation in tragedy of 'pity and fear, or terror . . . and such-like passions'. Given the vast variety of tragic works, subjects and treatments, it seems quite legitimate to enlarge Aristotle's list of emotional responses to tragedy, to suggest that it can also call forth awe, admiration, wonder, triumph, melancholy, despair, resignation, or any combination of these. The point to make about the vision one has at the end of any tragedy is that it is one of confusion, of bafflement, on the one hand, and of perception, on the other, and that contradictory feelings are often held in conjunction. It must be remembered, too, that Aristotle's views had their origin in his study of Greek plays, and can be applied only with large reservations to Shakespeare's. It is obvious that any attempt to rationalise a tragic ending is doomed to failure; one can never be quite sure that any two spectators or readers will respond in similar ways.

Bibliography: A. C. Bradley, *Shakespearian Tragedy*, 1904, Macmillan; C. Brooks, ed., *Tragic Themes in Western Literature*, 1955, Oxford University Press; H. D. F. Kitto, *Form and Meaning in Drama*, 1956, Methuen; T. R. Henn, *The Harvest of Tragedy*, 1956, Methuen, R. B. Sewall, *The Vision of Tragedy*, 1959, Oxford University Press; D. D. Raphael, *The Paradox of Tragedy*, 1960, Allen and Unwin, I. Ribnmer, *Patterns in Shakespearian Tragedy*, 1960, Methuen; F. L. Lucas, *Serious Drama in Relation to Aristotle's Poetics*, (1927), reprinted 1961; O. Mandel, *A Definition of Tragedy*, New York, 1961, New York University Press; J. Holloway, *The Story of the Night*, 1961, Routledge; G. Steiner, *The Death of Tragedy*, 1961, Faber; R. W. Corrigan, ed., *Tragedy: Vision and Form* Chicago, 1965, Chandler Publishing; C. Leech, ed., *Shakespeare: The Tragedies. A Collection of Critical Essays*, 1965, University of Chicago Publishers; D. W. Lucas, ed., *Aristotle's Poetics*, 1968, Oxford University Press; D. D. Krook, *Elements of Tragedy*, 1969, Yale University Press; C. Leech, *Tragedy*, 1969, Methuen; K. Muir, *Shakespeare's Tragic Sequence* , 1972, Hutchinson.

Wit and Humour

One standard dictionary defines wit as 'the felicitous association of objects not usually connected, so as to produce a pleasant surprise; also the power of readily combining objects in such a manner' (Webster). Like many literary terms, wit has changed its meaning; in the Renaissance it meant mind, intellect, understanding, sense; later usage has extended and developed its implications.

The witty writer or speaker seizes on some idea, situation or event and gives it a sudden turn, presenting it under new and unexpected aspects. The pleasure we derive from wit arises from the ingenuity of this turn, from the sudden surprise it brings, from our recognition of its sometimes odd appropriateness. In poetry, wit finds its characteristic expression in the conceit (see separate article) and the verse epigram. The latter is a short, concise and pithy composition which often, though not always, ends on a surprising note. Pope's tribute to Newton is a good example: 'Nature and nature's laws lay hid in night / God said, Let Newton be! and all was light'. Sometimes, verse epigrams are not formal compositions; many of the rhyming couplets of Pope and Dryden, for example, are self-contained epigrams ('See how the world its veterans rewards / A youth of folly and an age of cards'; 'Shadwell alone of all my sons is he / Who stands confirmed in full stupidy'). Witty epigrams are found in prose as well as in verse: the comedies of the Restoration and eighteenth century and the works of Wilde and Shaw are full of them; the *obiter dicta* of both the latter feature celebrated examples. Wilde's conversation sparkled with spontaneous effusions of witty comment mainly on conventional standards, his best effects being often achieved by changing a word or two in a common proverb or cliché: 'I can resist everything except temptation'; 'Work is the curse of the drinking classes'; 'One of those characteristic British faces that, once seen, are never remembered'. *The Importance of Being Earnest* is one of the wittiest plays ever written.

Wit became a central critical term in the early decades of

179

the twentieth century, mainly due to the influence of T. S. Eliot's use of it to describe some characteristic features of seventeenth-century Metaphysical poetry. In a celebrated essay on Marvell, Eliot admits the difficulty of attempting to 'translate the quality indicated by the dim and antiquated term wit into the equally unsatisfactory nomenclature of our own time'. Eliot's comments on Marvell and the other seventeenth-century Metaphysical poets convey his admiration for the fine fusion of intelligence and feeling found in their best poetry. He describes early seventeenth century wit as 'a tough reasonableness beneath the slight lyric grace' (*Selected Essays*, 1932, p. 293). And in a fine passage he remarks that, with our eye on Marvell, 'we can say that wit is not erudition; it is sometimes stifled by erudition, as in much of Milton. It is not cynicism, though it has a kind of toughness which may be confused with cynicism by the tender-minded. It is confused with erudition because it implies a constant inspection and criticism of experience. It involves, probably, a recognition, implicit in the expression of every experience, of other kinds of experience which are possible' (*Selected Essays*, p. 303). Basil Willey provides a useful comment on the last part of Eliot's statement when he suggests that the mind of a Metaphysical poet was not 'finally committed to any one world. Instead it could hold them all in a loose synthesis together, yielding itself, as only a mind in free poise can, to the passion of detecting analogies and correspondences between them' (*The Seventeenth Century Background*, 1934, pp. 42–3). Coleridge had already talked of wit as that 'which discovers partial likeness hidden in general diversity'.

To illustrate the peculiar quality of Metaphysical wit, Eliot examined Marvell's *To His Coy Mistress,* which has as its theme one of the great commonplaces of European literature: *carpe diem,* a theme found in such poems as Herrick's *Gather Ye Rosebuds* and Waller's *Go Lovely Rose.* But Marvell's wit, as Eliot remarks, renews the theme 'in a variety of concentrated images, each magnifying the original fancy'. And when this process has been completed, the poem turns with a series of arresting surprises of great imaginative power. The wit displayed in such poems as this is not, Eliot claims, 'the wit of Dryden, the great master of contempt, or of Pope, the great master of hatred, or of Swift, the great master of disgust . . .

You cannot find it in Shelley or Keats or Wordsworth
. . . still less in Tennyson or Browning' (*Selected Essays*, p. 293).
Eighteenth-century wit is less adventurous, less startling
than that of the seventeenth-century Metaphysicals. Their
constant search for far-fetched correspondences and analogies
was generally regarded in the eighteenth century as a gross
breach of decorum. No eighteenth-century poet would admit
an image like this one of Marvell's:

> And now the salmon-fishers moist
> Their leathern boats begin to hoist;
> And like Antipodes in shoes
> Have shod their heads in their canoes.
>
> (*Upon Appleton House*)

This would be seen by the eighteenth century as an example
of false wit. A famous eighteenth-century view is given by
Pope:

> True wit is Nature to advantage dressed
> What oft was thought, but ne'er so well expressed
> Something whose truth convinced at sight we find
> That gives us back the image of our mind
>
> (*Essay in Criticism*, 297ff)

It is interesting to note that the greatest of the eighteenth-
century critics, Samuel Johnson, disparaged both
Metaphysical wit and the account given by Pope. Johnson is
talking about the Metaphysical poets: "If Wit be well
described by Pope as being 'that which has been often
thought, but was never before so well expressed', they certainly never attained nor ever sought it, for they endeavoured to
be singular in their thoughts, and were careless of their diction. But Pope's account of wit is undoubtedly erroneous; he
depresses it below its natural dignity, and reduces it from
strength of thought to happiness of language. If by a more
noble and more adequate conception that be considered Wit
which is at once natural and new, that which though not obvious upon its first production, is acknowledged to be just; if it
be that, which he that never found it, wonders how he missed;
to wit of this kind the Metaphysical poets have seldom risen.

Their thoughts are often new, but seldom natural; they are not obvious, but neither are they just; and the reader, far from wondering that he missed them, wonders more frequently by what perverseness they were ever found' (*The Life of Cowley*).

Wit is, perhaps, not a quality entirely congenial to the English mind. Some of the wittest 'English' writers have really been Irishmen: Swift, Goldsmith, Sheridan, Wilde and Shaw, for example. Humour is a more characteristically English quality. In the sixteenth century, 'humour' denoted an unbalanced mental state, an unreasonable caprice, a fixed vice or folly. The peculiarities of the humorist (or eccentric person) were seen as fit subjects for comedy (whose main function was seen as the correction of irrational or immoral conduct). The great master of this kind of comedy (the comedy of humours) was Ben Jonson, many of whose greater characters are possessed, body and soul, by some single humour, dominated by a single ruling passion, and can never act except in conformity with this. The audience laughs as Jonson's great eccentrics manifest their whims and oddities to the point of absurdity. In *The Silent Woman,* a character called Morose is determined to eliminate all forms of noise from his life; this is his 'humour'. The very name of another character (in *The Alchemist*), Sir Epicure Mammon, indicates the nature of his humour: 'I will have all by beds blown up, not stuffed / Down is too hard / My meat shall all come in, in Indian shells / Dishes of agate set in gold, and studded / With emeralds, sapphires, hyacinths and rubies' (II, ii, 41 ff). Much English humour is at the expense of eccentric figures (not all of them by any means as unlikeable as Jonson's characters) whose oddities are liable to take any number of forms. Among English novelists, Sterne and Dickens are the great humorists. In a well-known story designed to caricature traditional English reserve, an Oxford student is represented as standing on the bank of a river, looking in helpless agitation at a drowning man and crying out: 'Oh that I had been *introduced* to this gentleman, that I might save his life'.

It is possible to distinguish between wit and humour in a variety of ways. Wit, as Northrop Frye remarks, 'is addressed to the awakened intelligence'. It is a form of intellectual quickness, raillery and repartee, and likely to be an upper-class manner of discourse. The dramatist Farquhar remarked in 1712 that 'the courtier cries out for wit, the citizen for humour'. Wit is potentially more dangerous a weapon than humour. It appeals to clever people; humour can find its way to the heart and feelings of even the least sophisticated. Wit, like any mental skill, presupposes learning and art; humour is a more spontaneous gift. Humour is a more natural, less studied and restrained an expression of character than wit. Wit is one of the most effective weapons of the satirist; humour is not a feature of satire. In a literary work, wit can flash forth in a single, isolated sentence whose force may be largely independent of the context (of speaker, time and place). The witty dramatist, for example, often runs the risk of putting his own witticisms into the mouths of all his characters, so that all of them appear equally clever. Humour, by contrast, must gather its strength from a larger context, taking into account the previous life of a character and the relationships between characters. It is an instructive comment on eighteenth-century polite taste that many critics of the earlier part of that century regarded humour as being inconsistent with true politeness, since the well-bred were supposed to have learned to repress their feelings and adapt their manners to a rigid code of decorum. But the late eighteenth and early nineteenth centuries saw the growth of a more tolerant attitude to humour as amusing, innocent, generous, benevolent, allied to sympathy and pathos; and of a less genial view of wit, now regarded as severe, bitter and harsh.

Other basic distinctions between wit and humour should be mentioned. Wit is verbal: only a saying or speech can be witty. One cannot talk of a witty situation or a witty appearance or a witty action; one can, on the other hand, describe a situation, appearance or action as humorous. A speech may be humorous as well as witty. A witty speech is epigrammatic and concise; a humorous one not necessarily so. A witty speaker is intentionally witty: he achieves his effects deliberately. Humour, on the other hand, may be unconscious. In the following exchange from *The Importance of Being Earnest*, Miss Prism's retort is humorous if it is not ironical:

Canon Chausible: The precept as well as the practice of the Primitive Church was distinctly against matrimony.

Miss Prism: That is obviously the reason why the
                         Primitive Church has not lasted up to
                         the present day.

Falstaff, Shakespeare's supreme comic creation, exhibits
both a ready wit and humour in all its aspects (in his appearance, his actions and his speeches). It can be claimed
without exaggeration that here, more than in any single
character, the whole range of comic possibilities is displayed.
Falstaff even defines his own standing as a comic character:
'Men of all sorts take a pride to gird at me. The brain of this
foolish compounded clay, man, is not able to invent anything
that intends to laughter more than I invent or is invented of
me. I am not only witty in myself, but the cause that wit is in
other men. I do here walk before thee like a sow that hath
overwhelmed all her litter but one' (*Henry IV*, Pt II, I, ii, 6 ff).
In his humorous aspects, Falstaff is the *miles gloriousus* (the
military braggart), but neither a liar nor a coward in the usual
sense. He is the archetypal parasite, the master of the revels
and Lord of Misrule. He has affinities with the Vice of the
Elizabethan morality plays (a tempter both sinister and
comic). He is the clown who can play many parts and even
stage a comic triumph over death. He is the quintessential
glutton, the comic fat man who 'lards the lean earth' as he
walks along. He is the buffoon who is at times a profound
critic of the values of his society. He is compounded of a whole
range of incongruities: old in years, he is psychologically little
more than a great baby; he is a dupe as well as a wit; harmless
and wicked; a liar without deceit; a knightly gentleman but
without dignity or honour; cowardly in appearance, braver in
reality.
    Falstaff's wit has been well described by Hazlitt. Its secret,
as that critic pointed out, is, 'for the most part, a masterly
presence of mind, an absolute self-possession, which nothing
can disturb'. Everybody has noticed his infinite capacity for
extricating himself from his predicaments, his delight in
creating dilemmas for himself so that he may enjoy disengag-
ing himself from them. A feature of his wit is its alacrity: his
mind is in complete control of his great body. He forgives the
Hostess for a crime she has not committed, and for this con-
descension she pawns all she has to lend him money, which he

makes a favour of accepting. He can shift responsibility for his
debts on to the backs of his creditors, as if the very size of these
debts made him proprietor of the inn ('Shall I take mine ease
in mine inn?').

It has already been pointed out that the meanings assigned
to such terms as wit and humour have varied with time. With
regard to humour, one modern development deserves at least
a brief mention. Traditionally, humour has been regarded as
kinder, less malicious, more tolerant than wit, and the
humorist as a comparatively genial observer of the human
comedy in contrast to, say, the satirist (compare, for example,
Fielding and Dickens with Swift or Shakespearian with
Jonsonian comedy). This account of humour needs to be
modified in the light of certain modern trends in drama and
fiction issuing in what is generally called, for want of a better
term, the literature of the absurd. The extent of the modifica-
tion will depend on one's view of the importance of these
trends. The best-known English-speaking writer in the 'ab-
surdist' tradition is Samuel Beckett. Both his drama and his
fiction exploit what is now widely known as black humour:
the exploitation for comic purposes of events and situations
which would normally be regarded with horror, revulsion or
pity. Beckett's works contain numerous memorable passages
of black humour. The situations in which his characters find
themselves may be painful, even hopeless; time and again,
however, he makes us laugh grimly with them as they reveal
the macabre or grotesque side of their predicament or that of
their fellow-sufferers. 'Nothing is funnier than unhappiness',
says one of the characters in *Endgame*. In the ironically named
Happy Days, the central character Winnie, is much diverted by
the thought of 'laughing wild amid severest woe'. Her optimistic gaiety, her constant use of 'wonderful' to describe
everything about her, the superficial levity of her comments,
are all in frightening contrast to the real horror of her plight.
In the novel *Watt*, several kinds of laughter are analysed,
among them 'the bitter laugh that laughs at that which is not
good' and the 'hollow laugh' which is also the intellectual
laugh; it laughs 'at that which is not true'. But the 'laugh or
laughs', the 'risus purus' is the one that has its source in 'that
which is unhappy'.

See separate articles on Comedy, Conceit and Metaphysical Poetry.

Bibliography: T. S. Eliot, *'Andrew Marvell'* in *Selected Essays,* 1932, Faber; F. R. Leavis, *Revaluation,* 1936, Chatto; H. B. Charlton, *Shakespearian Comedy,* 1938, Methuen; W. Empson, *The Structure of Complex Words,* 1951, Chatto; J. B. Leishman, *The Monarch of Wit,* 1951, Hutchinson; L. Cazamian, *The Development of English Humour,* 1952, Duke University Press; F. W. Sypher, ed., *Comedy,* 1956; A. Alvarez, *The School of Donne,* 1961, Chatto; G. Williamson, *The Proper Wit and Poetry,* 1961, Faber; V. Mercier, *The Irish Comic Tradition,* 1962, Oxford University Press; P. Lauter, *Theories of Comedy,* 1964, Doubleday; D. J. Milburn, *The Age of Wit, 1650–1750,* 1966, Macmillan, New York.

KING ALFRED'S COLLEGE
LIBRARY